Working Abroad with Purpose

Working Abroad with Purpose

The Way of a Tentmaker

GLENN D. DECKERT

Foreword by James Lundgren

WIPF & STOCK · Eugene, Oregon

WORKING ABROAD WITH PURPOSE
The Way of a Tentmaker

Copyright © 2019 Glenn D. Deckert. All rights reserved. Except for brief quotations in critical publications or reviews, no part of this book may be reproduced in any manner without prior written permission from the publisher. Write: Permissions, Wipf and Stock Publishers, 199 W. 8th Ave., Suite 3, Eugene, OR 97401.

Wipf & Stock
An Imprint of Wipf and Stock Publishers
199 W. 8th Ave., Suite 3
Eugene, OR 97401

www.wipfandstock.com

PAPERBACK ISBN: 978-1-5326-7455-6
HARDCOVER ISBN: 978-1-5326-7456-3
EBOOK ISBN: 978-1-5326-7457-0

Manufactured in the U.S.A.   FEBRUARY 1, 2019

All Scripture quotations, unless otherwise indicated, are taken from the Holy Bible, New International Version®, NIV®. Copyright © 1973, 1978, 1984, 2011 by Biblica, Inc.™ Used by permission of Zondervan. All rights reserved worldwide. www.zondervan.com. The "NIV" and "New International Version" are trademarks registered in the United States Patent and Trademark Office by Biblica, Inc.™

Scripture quotations marked ESV are from The Holy Bible, English Standard Version® (ESV®), copyright © 2001 by Crossway, a publishing ministry of Good News Publishers. Used by permission. All rights reserved.

Scripture quotations marked kjv are taken from the King James Version.

In gratitude and memory of my parents James and Norma Deckert
and
Ann's parents Al and Dorothy Oman
Who early taught us each to fear and love God.
They gave us their utmost support from the time we set off
On what was for them
An unconventional approach to serving Jesus Christ abroad.

Contents

Foreword by James Lundgren | ix
Preface | xiii
Acknowledgments | xv
Introduction | xvii

1. Tentmaking | 1
2. A Personal Account | 11
3. Finding Employment Abroad | 20
4. Obtaining Prayer Support | 28
5. Securing Visas and Permits | 32
6. Settling on Housing and Schooling | 35
7. Discovering Fellowship in the Host Country | 42
8. Seeing Opportunities for Outreach | 46
9. Confronting Issues in Language Learning | 54
10. Relating to Existing Ministries | 60
11. Benefiting from Local Employment | 64
12. Identifying Provision for Medical Care | 71
13. Having Income on Extended Home Stays | 76
14. Facing Unpredictable Material Crises and Retirement | 79
15. Limitations and Logistics | 85
16. Concluding Remarks | 91

Appendix | 101
Bibliography | 103

Foreword

ONE OF THE CENTRAL themes of God's Word, from beginning to end, is his plan to bless humanity through his people. We see it in Genesis 12 when God tells Abram that "all the peoples on earth will be blessed through you." We see God's desire to bless all of his creation in Jesus' encounters with the Canaanite women in Matthew 15 and the Samaritan women at the well in John 4, in the conversion of hundreds of people from all over the known world in Acts 2 and in Paul's ministry to the gentiles. From the beginning of the early church, God's people have obeyed his call to bless the world by following the tentmaking example of the apostle Paul. They crossed cultures using their vocational calling and training to give them direct access to countries and people groups on their "turf" through service and witness.

In my forty-plus years of service in campus ministry through InterVarsity/USA, I have had the joy of being part of God's call to hundreds of undergraduate and graduate students and faculty members to ministry opportunities all over the world. Some have gone through a mission agency with the prayer and financial support of churches and individuals. Others have used their vocational training to fund themselves and serve Christ globally in spheres of education, business, medicine, and through relief agencies. As I have encouraged, prayed for, and supported these brothers and sisters, it has been a huge blessing for me to see their love for the people they are serving and partnering with, their dedication to their work, and the way God has worked in them and through them as they have, again and again, said yes to God's call.

Many times, as graduating students have come to me to ask about tentmaking mission opportunities, I have wished for a resource like *Working Abroad with Purpose*. As I read through the book, I realize that this was exactly what they needed, and I was doubly excited about it for two reasons.

First, there are few people who I respect more than Glenn and Ann Deckert. They had a significant role in my coming to faith while I was studying at the University of Illinois in 1969. Their dedication to Christian disciplines and the men and women that Glenn introduced me to in the U of I InterVarsity chapter all combined through the work of the Holy Spirit to transform my life. As a squirrely, rebellious and adrift freshman, I saw the emptiness of my current path. Through the consistent witness that they and those fellow students exhibited day in and day out, I fell in love with Jesus and he called me home. As you read *Working Abroad with Purpose*, you see how Glenn and Ann lived that same way in each country and in each of the vocational and neighborhood settings that God led them to as tentmaking missionaries.

Second, as I read the book, I was hit again and again with the way the Scriptures and biblical values weaved their way into the way Glenn and Ann served in each setting. It is one thing for a book like this to thoroughly cover all the practical issues that someone exploring tentmaking ministry will need to face, which it does quite well. It is even better when the practical issues are dealt with concretely but always through the lens of what Scripture teaches about vocational integrity and missions. For example, the tension between the two priorities of evangelism and vocational excellence are explored and lived out without losing one or the other. One can easily see the priority the Deckerts put on integrity, excellence, and hospitality in the universities where Glenn taught and in the neighborhoods where they lived. This was not a technique or an empty strategy. This was an outgrowth of who they were and are as followers of Christ. At the same time, they never lost sight of the fact that God had called them to do the work of

Foreword

evangelism and discipleship with non-Christians and Christians that they encountered. All through the book, you see the way those two priorities lived in harmony wherever God brought them.

Additionally, the reader will be blessed by all that is shared about the ups and downs that the Deckerts went through as one door shut in a university or country and they then had to look to God to open another opportunity elsewhere. For many of us, that process would have been overwhelming. It would have been easy to question God's goodness and direction and move away from his call. Clearly, the reader can see that some of those transitions were a great challenge for Glenn and Ann. Through it all though, they chose to trust in the sovereignty and provision of God and, without hesitation, engage on the process of seeking the next opportunity.

All of that is why this is an excellent book for anyone who is considering a life of tentmaking ministry. No practical issue is ignored or left out and the wisdom is invaluable. But it is also a profound book about living the Christian life with dedication and faithfulness wherever God takes you geographically or vocationally. In the spirit of many of the missionary biographies, every Christian who reads this book will experience a significant encouragement to greater faithfulness and service to Christ in whatever locale God has placed them.

JAMES LUNDGREN
Senior Vice President of Collegiate Ministries
Interim President of IVCF/USA

Preface

DURING OUR RETIREMENT YEARS, Ann and I are now seldom engaged directly in ministry abroad. Instead, we often listen to the stories of younger folks who are preparing for overseas service or who are reflecting upon their own first several years serving abroad. Some are dealing with frustration over slow-moving fundraising, or even recent loss of donor support, and some appear discouraged over doors closing to the field of their choice. A few tell us they were summoned and told to leave and were no longer welcome where they had invested their last several years. In response to their sharing, I have sometimes said to myself, "If only he/she knew about . . ." So, a couple years ago on a week-long, lakeside vacation site I began drafting on the notion of tentmaking and how it leads qualified people to open doors for Christian witness abroad—and with little, if any, need for fundraising. It seemed so few had ever gotten a clear understanding of what tentmaking is all about. How could these people ever consider seriously the tentmaking strategy for Christian witness abroad if they never heard of it—or had only heard a questionable representation of the approach? With the passing of several more months, I decided it was time for me to write more in earnest.

From the outset, I wanted to write to inform a younger generation of candidates, both students and young professionals, whose hearts are set on service abroad as God may guide them. And what I write should be of interest to retirees who are keen to serve the Lord with their skills and livable pension. I was not particularly

Preface

interested in approaching the topic academically for the critique and debate of missiologists. Already many thinkers on missionary strategy had debated and formed ideas on tentmaking. Some aspiring missionary candidates had already come across splendid articles or essays on tentmaking, many written by Ruth Siemens. Yet, to the best of my knowledge, no book-size presentation on historic tentmaking and its outworking had been published over the previous twenty years. I felt what Ann and I had experienced in our two decades of living abroad as tentmakers might be helpful to others.

The challenge I faced was drawing selectively and accurately from our own experience abroad while incorporating what I was finding in earlier books and articles on various notions of tentmaking. I wanted to produce something highly illustrated, thoroughly practical, comprehensive, and yet concise to address the questions a new generation of volunteers might be asking about service abroad as a tentmaker. It gradually dawned on me that my audience might not be only North American readers, but also readers in the Majority World where newly founded churches and church associations are hammering out their own missionary sending programs, but often with limited financial resources.

As for accuracy of detail on what I recall from our past experiences, I discovered the great value of my packs of old diary notes stored away in a bulging cardboard carton. Where I had to rely more on memory, Ann's recall sometimes sharpened and often confirmed my own. Some of the quotations in stories that follow are my best recollection and formulation of words when spoken so significantly impacted me that they are virtually unforgettable. Other quotations were written communications buried away in paper files until brought to light as they appear in the following accounts. Having put these pieces together into one small volume, even if only a few readers gain helpful insight and inspiration to give serious attention to the tentmaking model, I will have accomplished my foremost purpose.

Acknowledgements

I WOULD BE REMISS not to extend credit and thanks to many people who kindly helped move my drafting forward eventually into publication. First, I thank Ann, my wife, for much more than her encouragement and input into this final product. She's the one who set up our comfortable living quarters in so many communities abroad and under such different and sometimes challenging conditions. She gladly welcomed so many guests into our home, prepared so many meals to serve others, cared so diligently for our two growing children, and has always been my closest prayer partner. If to some extent I have lived the life of a New Testament Aquila, she has been the faithful Priscilla and even more. As for this book on tentmaking, she carefully read many early drafts for corrections and helpful suggestions. Our two children, Natalie and James, often gave reassuring words to press on with the project believing "Dad's book" would for sure benefit others.

Many people helped with the structure, content, and language of this book. Thanks first to Ruth Hubbard of InterVarsity whose resourcefulness through our correspondence provided valuable suggestions, once on the scope of my claims, another time on the best focus of the manuscript, and always with a word of encouragement. I'm indebted to John Maust who read an early draft and worked with me on the layout of the material I wanted to share. Mark Canada gave helpful suggestions on matters of language and style. My esteemed colleague, Tom Scovel, gave helpful corrections and pointers on what more might be included on language

Acknowledgements

learning. Others who read early drafts commended the project and gave worthy recommendations. These include Jim and Carol Plueddemann, Chet Wood, Jeremy Taylor, and Wayne and Cindy Shabaz. Thanks to Steve Board whose long experience in publishing was a frequent source of help. Special thanks to long-term friend and mentor Ed Jaeger, and late wife Belle, who years ago in Iran modeled for Ann and me the way of authentic tentmaking.

I remain indebted to so many, and to those who faithfully supported us through prayer during our many years abroad. Jerry and Carolyn Norquist were not only devout prayer supporters, but were our helping hands on the home front when we were far away. Cliff and Priscilla Christians so kindly kept their home open to us on our many return visits to Champaign/Urbana. In working with Wipf and Stock personnel in the last stages, typesetter George Callihan was especially helpful. Above all, I give thanks to God who sustained Ann and me in our many situations and gave us our reason for settling abroad. May this account in some small way help to further our Lord's kingdom.

Introduction

DRAWING ON TWO DECADES of residence and employment in several countries as a follower of Jesus Christ, I delight in sharing the world of possibilities lying before those who contemplate bearing witness to Christ abroad as tentmakers. A tentmaker is a skilled employable layperson who accepts a job in his/her area of expertise in a particular society abroad in order to glorify God through exemplary job performance and diligent sharing of the gospel with others in that setting. The tentmaker's job covers his/her expenses and possibly expenses of others laboring in that same setting. The job also provides a network of relationships with nationals for friendship and witness. Taking one's professional training and skills abroad in this fashion for cross-cultural witness to people not yet informed of the gospel is a legitimate and rewarding career option.

A tentmaker lives with a sense of calling to a particular vocation and its role in society. Every legitimate vocation contributes in some way to society's functioning, betterment, and well-being. As Martin Luther and other reformers maintained, the calling of the farmer, banker, craftsman, mother, and homemaker is a sacred facet of the divine plan for mankind. All who come to know God, both laypeople and clergy, are to work out their holy calling in the light of the Christian gospel and scriptural teaching, and in that calling find meaning and fulfillment. A calling and commitment to a particular vocation in no way detracts from a commitment

Introduction

to spreading the gospel and discipling new believers. Rather, the vocation helps to locate the person's efforts in furthering the good news. Consequently, a tentmaker adheres to both a vocation and the commission of Jesus Christ to spread the gospel and make disciples. Gary Ginter, in a chapter entitled "Overcoming Resistance through Tentmaking," comments: "The most effective tentmaking springs from the melding of the Great Commission and the theology of work as vocation.... Effective tentmakers know that God is pleased to see them do their work well."[1] Accordingly, a tentmaker aims to be an asset to his/her own professional discipline and to others who practice it. At the same time, in respect to the Great Commission, the tentmaker is eager to make Jesus Christ known in the workplace and among all those he/she encounters in the adopted country. The tentmaker cannot afford to be a minimalist in respect to either the vocation or the gospel, but rather diligently pursues both.

In today's global economy, tentmaking as a career option for cross-cultural Christian witness is too often totally unknown, misunderstood, or just left unexamined by an upcoming generation that is committed to Christian ministry abroad. A clear understanding of its outworking is equally distant from most Christians who are already employed outside their own country. While across the globe doors open and close for traditional missionary endeavors, Christian workers must see the growing opportunity for Christians with relevant qualifications to fill open positions of employment in scores of countries—whether those countries welcome traditional missionary activity or not. Positions abroad offer daily access to nationals for personal friendship and Christian witness. The most marketable skill sets needed to fill job openings abroad may vary over time and from place to place as countries develop, but today's tentmakers representing a wide range of disciplines and skills are sure to find acceptable positions in target countries of choice by means of a careful job search.

It is my hope that you the reader will grasp the concept of taking your vocational skills abroad for strategic positioning to

---

1. Ginter, "Overcoming Resistance," 211.

Introduction

advance God's kingdom. Toward that end, in chapters 3 through 14 I set forth twelve areas in which a determined tentmaker is sure to discover God's provision and enablement as my wife and I experienced over our years abroad as tentmakers. My hope and prayer is that as you read these pages, God will help you sense whether your own calling, gifting, and character point toward a tentmaking career as you learn more about this option.

1

Tentmaking
The Concept and Practice

ORIGIN AND EXAMPLES OF TENTMAKING

THE TERM "TENTMAKING" IS derived from the life and ministry of the apostle Paul who often used his vocational training of making tents from goatskins to pay for his living and ministry expenses. The tents he made were a useful marketable product for people of his day. Tentmaking today means using one's professional skills to render products or services as a means of livelihood in a cross-cultural situation with the aim of sharing the gospel with others. Several Old Testament characters like Joseph and Daniel bore witness to the God of Abraham, Isaac, and Jacob when in the employ of pagan kings far from their own homeland, but they were not in those roles of service by choice.

By contrast, the apostle Paul, in response to God's call to carry the gospel to the gentile world, often relied on his tentmaking skill to provide for his needs while fulfilling God's commission. He did this for extended periods in Corinth (Acts 18:3), Ephesus (Acts 20:34), and Thessalonica (1 Thess 2:9; 2 Thess 3:8-9). Undoubtedly, he had learned his trade during his upbringing in a Jewish home the way all Jewish boys learned some trade in their youth.

Working Abroad with Purpose

In his missionary travels, he not only provided for his own needs through this means, but the needs of his companions in ministry as well (Acts 20:33-34).

Paul did not always depend exclusively on this means of income. Clearly, he received donations from believers in Philippi (Phil 4:15-16) and may have had other unmentioned sources of financial support. Yet, from all that we know about the apostle Paul, he never solicited funds for himself from any of the churches he established nor from his base in Antioch, much less in the modern sense of raising sustained donor support for the long haul. The very thought of him doing so seems totally out of character for him and contrary to what we know about his readiness to preempt any charge that he was a peddler of some new teaching for pay. Instead, we see in the New Testament not only Paul but others, like Priscilla and Aquila, who simply shared their faith wherever they went while providing for their own needs through their ordinary means of livelihood. These New Testament characters had no need to practice their trades in order to gain entry to a "limited access" region as is sometimes the strategy today in light of the fact that many countries now restrict or forbid the entry of traditional missionaries. The apostle simply used his training and trade to meet his living and ministry expenses as he moved along spreading the gospel.

In recent times, J. Christy Wilson Jr. (1921-1999) effectively promoted the tentmaking model at a time when an increasing number of countries had closed their doors, or were slowly closing them, to traditional donor-supported missionaries. Wilson's *Today's Tentmakers* aimed to seize the attention of new missionary candidates and awaken the church at large and the missionary establishment of that time to a world of opportunity through tentmaking. The book's subtitle succinctly stated Wilson's thesis. It read, *Self-support: An Alternative Model for Worldwide Witness*. He reviewed in detail both the biblical basis for tentmaking and the many historical precedents from the early Christian centuries leading up to many examples in the eighteenth and nineteenth centuries. He gave special attention to William Carey (1761-1834) who is recognized widely as "The Father of Modern Missions." After Carey arrived in India and his financial support from England dwindled, he relied upon his skill as a shoemaker to cover his expenses. He went on to support himself and others through managing an indigo plantation, involvement in a printing operation, and finally, through an academic position in Calcutta. His underlying passion, however, was advancing the gospel.

Wilson also referred to leading evangelicals of his day who gave enthusiastic support to the tentmaking model. His book tells the story of his own entry into the "closed" country of Afghanistan where he spent twenty-one years.[1] Closely following Wilson's publication, two other works provided practical help for those who wished to adopt the historic tentmaking approach to Christian witness abroad. These were Don Hamilton's *Tentmakers Speak: Practical Advice from Over 400 Missionary Tentmakers*, and Jonathan Lewis' edited volume, *Working Your Way to the Nations*.

More recent publications in missiology, like Patrick Lai's *Tentmaking: Business as Missions* (2005), portray tentmaking as morphing into what is now known as Business as Mission (BAM). Basically, advocates of BAM encourage the setting up of profit-making businesses, often in countries relatively closed to traditional missionary work, to offer employment to select team members and many nationals while providing a product or service to the local community. The company aims to operate according to biblical principles and provide a Christian witness in the community while being a means of economic development and social transformation. Lai's later volume, *Business for Transformation* (2015), is a virtual handbook on starting a business abroad.

C. Neal Johnson explains what a BAM business aims to do in his exhaustive work on BAM: "It creates jobs that pay wages, that gives [sic] people purchasing power, which in turn stimulates the economy by helping produce profits for other businesses."[2] He further explains that a BAM company has multiple bottom lines: "Briefly, these bottom lines are the financial, social, environmental

---

1. Wilson, *Today's Tentmakers*, 41–57.
2. Johnson, *Business as Mission*, 268.

and kingdom bottom lines."³ BAM can be viewed as a specialized type of historic tentmaking undertaken by Christians with proven business experience, sufficient investment capital, and a multi-year perspective on establishing such a profit-making business. By contrast, tentmakers of the historic kind find job openings in the target country—openings not of their own making—and make application. When offered an acceptable contract, they accept the position as their source of livelihood and their footing for Christian witness to nationals from the time they arrive in their adopted country.

I maintain that as a tentmaker you become engaged in a legitimate missionary role by moving from your own cultural setting to impact a workplace and community abroad through exemplary job performance and timely sharing of the gospel message. The employment abroad may be either in a local indigenous institution or, alternatively, in a global organization already planted in the target country. Employment there provides all, or practically all, of your living and ministry expenses. Some tentmakers use any other sources of funding they may have for less visible expenditures like insurance premiums, savings for retirement, or other needs in the homeland, but not to live at a higher standard of living than what their local salary enables. You aim to live on the scale of nationals holding similar employment while maintaining a distinctly Christian lifestyle. Your goal is to live and work in a way that is pleasing to God and winsome to fellow workers, neighbors, and friends. You see all of public life as a platform for authentic witness to Jesus Christ, the crucified, risen Savior and Lord. The website of Global Intent, formerly Global Opportunities, cites founder Ruth Siemens, once a tentmaker herself and later inspirer of many others to take up the tentmaking challenge: "Tentmakers are missions-motivated Christians who support themselves as they do cross-cultural evangelism on the job and in their free time."⁴

As summarized by Danny Martin, who was a key player in the rise of tentmaking internationally, missions-minded people of

3. Johnson, *Business as Mission*, 271.
4. Siemens, "What's Tentmaking?."

several nationalities with similar vision came together in Manila in 1989 and formed an organization now known as Tentmakers International Exchange (TIE). That was the beginning of a movement that gained momentum and sponsored international conferences in major cities of the world in 1997, 1999, and 2002. In the promotion of the movement, they developed resources, agreed on standards, appointed national leaders for the represented countries, and explored ways to offer training to would-be tentmakers.[5] A more detailed review of this early development of the movement is available in an article by John Cox.[6] Clearly, tentmaking is now an international movement composed of many national organizations. Most of this activity took place after my own long-term tentmaking commitments had ended. Certainly, today's tentmakers can benefit greatly from these developments and resources, especially in preparation for their ministry in a different cultural setting. The reader is advised to refer to the appendix for contact with helpful organizations.

A crucial question confronting a would-be tentmaker is how to pursue his/her vision in a foreign setting with some degree of companionship and team work. Tentmakers, in general, need partnership as most all cross-cultural workers do. Some tentmakers go abroad as a team drawn from a particular church. Some begin as a member of a missionary agency or, if unaffiliated, by accepting a measure of partnership with workers belonging to one or more established missionary agencies. Others join Christ-followers already in the same host country working as tentmakers. The experience of many tentmakers shows that the long-term pursuit of one's vision for the host country requires partnership in the field as well as prayer support in the homeland.

Ann, my wife, was my principal companion in our tentmaking undertakings from the time we set out for Tehran in 1970 until we agreed to return to the U.S. for long-term stateside employment in 1993. She also accompanied me as she was able in my later shorter appointments for the upgrading of English teaching

5. Martin, "History."
6. Cox, "Tentmaking Movement," 111–17.

in other countries. There were a few exceptions. For part of a five-month appointment to Qatar in 2002, and much of the 2005–06 academic year that I spent in Azerbaijan, she was unable to accompany me except for short periods due to other commitments back home. During all the other years of residence abroad we regularly planned, prayed, and served together. Especially in the use of our home for hospitality and meals at our dinner table she was the indispensable factor. Further, in times of seeming setback and discouragement she was to me a constant source of encouragement, insight, and joy. God, in fact, provided us with other supporting friendships in the various places we lived. Yet, little of what I report on our years of living abroad would have worked out very well without her constant partnership. For such a faithful and gifted companion, I am indescribably thankful to God.

UNDERLYING IMPLICATIONS OF TENTMAKING

Tentmaking, like all workplace ministries, represents a departure from the Old Testament conception of priestly service being limited to a minority of the people of Israel, the Levites, who were charged with conducting the formal priestly service for all the others. According to the Mosaic law, only designated priests were to conduct sacrifices and lead the worship centered in the tabernacle and later in the temple. Their work on behalf of the rest of the community was sustained by the material support of all the others. The Levites were to have no land of their own or means of income and were fully dependent upon the rest of the community for their sustenance.

A radical change in this arrangement is seen in the New Testament. The startling change comes in the pronouncement of Jesus in the Gospels and the practice of the early Christians as narrated in the book of Acts. The shift to an empowered laity is seen across the New Testament letters. Most decisive was the utterance of Jesus to the eleven disciples hours before he ascended: ". . . Go and make disciples of all nations, baptizing them . . . and teaching them to obey everything I have commanded you" (Matt

28:19–20). That was final; Matthew had nothing more to add to his account. So the small band of skilled fishermen, a former tax collector, and a growing number of commoners crossed the borders of Israel and moved on throughout the Roman world making disciples of gentiles as well as of Jews. This involved a shocking reorientation for the original disciples who, as Jews, for centuries had kept themselves separate from people of other races except for foreigners pressed into servitude and the occasional Rahab or Ruth featured in Old Testament stories. Jesus put an end to both Jewish exclusiveness and restricted priestly service.

That Jesus promised his personal presence to accompany his followers in carrying out this mission until the end of the age means that his presence remains with all who carry out the mission up to and including today. There is no evidence that Jesus' commissioning pertained only to the first apostles or merely a subset of religious leaders as some have argued. In the early centuries, whether out of sheer obedience to his command or in response to the promptings of the Holy Spirit, believers of all stations of life spread the faith across the Roman Empire in the face of resistant paganism, state-sponsored persecution, and hostile adherents of Judaism. The first Jewish believers and, increasingly, believers of other ethnicities found themselves involved in the spread of the gospel by virtue of their allegiance to Jesus and the empowerment of the Holy Spirit. This work of spreading the gospel was carried out without regard to formal qualifications. At the same time, it is clear in the New Testament that Christian teachers and evangelists were recognized and to some extent remunerated for their service to the church. Paul, in his first letter to the church in Corinth, made a strong case for apostles, including himself, having a right to material support for their ongoing labors for Christ's kingdom. Yet Paul largely chose to forego financial support to preempt any false charge that he was motivated by personal financial gain (1 Cor 9).

Scholars have studied just how it was that the Christian faith spread so rapidly across the Roman Empire against such odds. Michael Green, once rector in Oxford, England and author on the early church, in his analysis of this phenomenon, concludes: "Christianity was from its inception a lay movement, and so it continued for a remarkably long time . . . It appears the faith spread through informal chattering to friends and chance acquaintances, in homes and wine shops, on walks, and around market stalls."[7] Church historian Adolf Harnack discussed the agents of the spreading faith over the first three centuries giving due attention to the original apostles, prophets, teachers, and roving missionaries without reliable income as well as the outreach endeavors of the presbyters, bishops, regular clergy, and the early theologians. But he did not see any one of these as the chief agent in the spread of the Christian faith. He rather concluded that "the great mission of Christianity was in reality accomplished by means of informal missionaries."[8] Similarly, renowned Yale University church historian, Kenneth Scott Latourette, concluded that by the end of the third century, "The chief agents in the expansion of Christianity appear not to have been those who made it a profession or made it a major part of their occupation, but men and women who earned their livelihood in some purely secular manner and spoke of their faith to those whom they met in this natural fashion."[9]

These historians came to the same conclusion that the majority of those who carried out the Great Commission were ordinary believers, not salaried or benevolently supported workers. Biographies of missionary greats of the nineteenth and twentieth centuries may give the impression that the Christian faith generally spread abroad through funding from home country churches and generous individuals. Yet, research has concluded that the vast majority of witnesses to Christ in the spread of the Christian faith from the earliest times have been ordinary people who provided for their own material needs. These believers shared the gospel with family members, neighbors, colleagues, and clients wherever they went. In this manner, some crossed national borders to carry the gospel to other localities as did the many foreign visitors in

---

7. Green, *Evangelism*, 173.
8. Harnack, *Mission and Expansion*, 368.
9. Latourette, *A History of Expansion*, 116.

Tentmaking

Jerusalem who heard Peter boldly proclaim that Jesus, once crucified, had risen from the tomb (Acts 2). These returned to their own countries as did the Ethiopian eunuch who had learned the good news from Philip early in his return trip to his own country in Africa (Acts 8).

Unfortunately, today in many churches in the West, and in the churches they have helped plant elsewhere, is the widespread notion that the major work of the church in teaching, preaching, and evangelizing is inherently the work of a professional class of Christian workers. Perhaps unconsciously, churches have tended to revert to the Levitical practice of ancient Israel, the system in which a minority was materially supported by the many for priestly services for the whole community. It appears that many Protestant churches now, while giving lip service to the priesthood of all believers, as championed by Martin Luther and other reformers five hundred years ago, have slipped back to a clergy-dominated practice of ministry. By professionalizing Christian service and ministry, churches have—in effect—reduced a huge portion of the laity to observer status. Most devout laypeople financially and prayerfully support the ongoing work of the church at home and abroad, but they themselves participate largely in sustained outreach only vicariously. They have become accustomed to the notion that only a small subset of believers is adequately trained and equipped for explaining the gospel to outsiders and giving instruction on the application and outworking of the gospel in daily life.

Tentmakers are a part of a likely minority in the church with a different outlook. They see ordinary laypeople employed in many realms of society as people capable of assuming, with some encouragement and mentoring, many Word-centered ministries within the church and beyond. More importantly, by their daily give and take in a largely non-Christian pluralistic world, laypeople are the most uniquely informed and positioned to communicate the gospel in the terms and idiom of non-believers outside the church. Certainly not all lay witnesses to Christ are expected to move out cross-culturally as tentmakers, but all are called to be witnesses wherever they live and work.

Working Abroad with Purpose

Tentmakers imagine millions of ordinary believers fulfilling the Great Commission right where they have come to faith or later settled—tens of thousands of these under the guidance of the Holy Spirit fulfilling the commission cross-culturally in foreign lands, all without placing financial burden upon their home churches. That is, tentmaking represents a recovery of the practice of the church of the early centuries enhanced by today's ease of travel and ready access to myriads of helpful teaching resources. At the same time, tentmakers themselves recognize that the church's professionally trained clergy—prophets, evangelists, pastors, and teachers—provide much of the necessary preaching and teaching for the instruction and equipping of the laity (Eph 4:11–13). They agree that traditional missionaries relying on donor support are still needed to provide theological education abroad where doors remain open. Further, donor-supported missionaries are essential for tribal language analysis and description, Bible translation, literacy work, and for most pioneer work in primitive societies where options for employment and self-support do not exist.

2

A Personal Account

PREPARATION FOR A MISSIONARY CAREER

MY OWN ENTRY INTO a tentmaking career unfolded gradually as I sought out many possible sources of guidance for cross-cultural ministry. In my early adult years, I was not very familiar with the tentmaking concept and I knew of no self-declared tentmaker. I was reared by practicing Christian parents who had no overseas experience. Having made a commitment to serve as a foreign missionary, I took all the usual steps in preparing for a conventional missionary career with full parental approval: four years of undergraduate study followed by graduate study, earnest conversations with returned missionaries, and serious discussion with mission-board recruitment staff. As a student at Christian institutions of learning, I pursued various outlets of practical Christian service and personal witness to others in and beyond those places of formal study.

During undergraduate studies at Houghton College in western New York, I began to sense a drag on my own discipleship commitment and plans for missionary service. It traces back to when I turned sixteen and was engaged in my teenage dream of converting an old Model A Ford pickup truck into a custom-built two-seat convertible roadster shaped along the lines of the fashionable Ford Thunderbird of that time. My father allowed me access to his shop's machines and welding equipment, a retired auto mechanic neighbor gave me helpful tips, several automobile scrap yards let me hunt for useful parts, and a metal-working business friend of my family gave a few Saturdays at his shop to cut and roll large pieces of sheet metal for the car body I had designed. As the roadster was taking shape, I imagined the heads that would turn when I drove my unique vehicle into the college campus for my junior year at Houghton.

Then, an inner sense of misplaced priorities grew stronger with an increasing sense of unease. I heard God's quiet whisper, "Do you love me more than your car?" My rationalization on how this roadster could be useful in my friendships and witness to others failed to address that question, "Do you love me more than your car?" So after a lot of personal struggle and self-examination over a couple of weeks, shortly after my twentieth birthday, I swapped my roadster at one of Detroit's many used car dealerships for a very ordinary seven-year old sedan to drive back to college that fall. That was my hard but decisive answer to that quiet whisper. I was greatly relieved! I had no regret, even when an uncle told me he spotted my roadster in the car dealer's show window to attract attention. I have often looked back on that move as the decisive step sealing my commitment to Jesus Christ as I sought to know his will for my future.

The following summer prior to my senior year at Houghton I made an eight-week solo trip to Haiti, Colombia, and Ecuador—at a total cost of less than four hundred dollars at that time—to visit a few missionary families supported by my home church. I contracted to drive a new car to its purchaser in Tennessee and hitchhiked the rest of the way to Miami arriving in time for my Pam Am Airways flight to Haiti. I traveled with one stuffed duffle bag and a pad of twenty-dollar traveler's checks in my pocket. Experiencing a case of malaria in Haiti, harrowing bus rides over Colombia's mountain ranges, bumbling along in Colombia with my high-school Spanish, spending some nights in hostels for

A Personal Account

as little as fifty cents a night, being stopped by police for body searches, and following fellow bus passengers on river launches to board an awaiting bus to continue onward all made for a complete cross-cultural experience. When riding across Haiti with a couple of missionaries to attend a weekend regional church conference, I was struck by the many Haitian children along the dusty roadside with bloated stomachs and reddish hair from serious malnutrition. In Colombia, one missionary in particular, a big strapping Western Canadian, filled my mind with possibilities. Riding with him on a train to another city, I remember him gesturing out the window to stretches of fertile land and saying how he could farm that land for a great return for his educational ministry with peasants. I did my best to help my missionary hosts in various manual tasks and was given a few short speaking assignments at gatherings in which I read from my corrected Spanish script or spoke with the help of a translator.

At home during another summer of my seminary years, a missions-minded layman fifteen years my senior often met with me for sharing and prayer. One summer, week after week, we met early on Saturday mornings at a public park in Detroit to cook eggs and bacon on a small stove and share as we ate and prayed for God's leading in my life. Several times he took me along house-to-house in a Detroit neighborhood to share the gospel and our Christian experience with those who came to the door. Sometimes he took me to a public park to share something from Scripture with Sunday afternoon picnickers. These outreach ventures taught me things I could never learn in seminary classrooms.

With a deepening commitment to foreign missions I completed an MA degree in New Testament at Wheaton College and then the further requirements for the MDiv degree at Trinity Evangelical Divinity School (TEDS). As a student at Christian colleges and seminary, I was particularly involved in different capacities in chapters of the Foreign Missions Fellowship, an affiliate of InterVarsity Christian Fellowship (IVCF). This involved praying for missionaries, teaching on missions, and challenging fellow students to get involved in world missions.

Working Abroad with Purpose

My earliest reading that sparked in my thinking some aspects of the tentmaking model was in the 1960s when I came across a series of short readings by Roland Allen under the title "The Case for Voluntary Clergy" in a volume entitled *Ministry of the Spirit*, writings that first appeared in 1930. About the same time, a furloughed missionary from Brazil challenged me to look into a publication from Pan American Airways featuring English-medium universities in the developing world. I recall asking the missionary how that might figure into my next steps, and he simply replied with something like, "There are many possibilities, maybe study, maybe teaching—just see how God might lead." I found that publication, pored over it, and imagined how I might fit into an overseas university.

As I was finishing at TEDS, Paul Little, a professor of evangelism, suggested I consider doing full-time campus evangelism while waiting for clarity on overseas ministry. It was during the following four years of donor-supported campus evangelism and discipleship training with InterVarsity that Ann and I were married. Ann was an elementary school teacher at the time and had not thought seriously of foreign missionary service. She soon was aware of my strong pull toward overseas ministry and was comfortable with that. Two years after marrying, while I was still involved in InterVarsity campus work, we were searching for overseas study or work opportunities to give us a footing for overseas ministry. The country of Iran had captured my attention through two close friends who had spent time in that country, one assigned there for many months by an American electric power company and the other, a career missionary at that time, involved in Bible translation.

While doing InterVarsity campus work at the University of Illinois, I learned that same university offered an MA degree in Teaching English as a Second Language. In 1969, I enrolled in that program for full-time study while Ann supported us through a local teaching job that opened up for her in answer to our prayers. Just months before completing that degree, the university formally announced a new joint program with Tehran University requiring a team of newly minted teachers of English language. For us, this was a striking answer to our prayers, and I signed on to join the team of newly trained teachers drawn from several midwestern universities to teach English to students at Iran's most prestigious university for a livable stipend.

OUR FIRST TENTMAKING EXPERIENCE

So, in late summer 1970, we said goodbye to parents and friends including many prayer supporters and set off for Iran, by air to Europe and over land by bus from Munich, Germany to Tehran. The six-day bus ride across Communist countries and over dusty and rutted roads in Turkey was our way of getting both of us there on the equivalent of a single airfare ticket that my internship position provided. The long ride gave us acquaintance with several Iranians returning home from Europe, with an Iranian general accompanying his college-age daughter back to Iran, and a nurse from England, as well as with several adventurous backpackers. A mechanical breakdown in eastern Turkey, at a site giving us a panoramic view of Mount Ararat, was a most memorable event. Our eventual transfer to a set of minibuses for the last stretch to the Iranian border ended the delay but soon led to a problem with the minibus we were on. Between the rear wheels, a set of leaf springs came apart. The driver solved that by calling for one of the women to surrender a nylon stocking which he used to tightly wrap together the separated metal straps. We were soon back on our way to the Iranian border.

After five years of language teaching in Iran and finding ways to share our faith with local people, we returned to the University of Illinois so I could pursue a PhD to enhance my professional prospects in Iran. A graduate program along my areas of interest in education allowed me to focus on literacy and learning in developing countries. In the summer of 1977 I interviewed samples of bank managers, engineers, shop owners, and teachers in Iran for writing a dissertation on the status of adult voluntary reading in a country where for centuries oral communication was primary. After completing the degree, Ann and I, with six-year-old daughter and two-month-old son, returned to Iran for a position in the more remote city of Kerman. We soon learned we were the only American family with children living in the city. For a few months I watched my new university worksite become a disordered hotbed of political debate and conflict over the Shah and his policies. Tanks were moving into the streets amid throngs of angry protestors, and night after night we lay in bed hearing the sound of gunfire and sirens. In the mornings, when out on the streets, we discovered what further liquor shops or movie theaters had been broken into and set ablaze. Our plans for the future similarly went up in smoke. The Iranian revolution brought our work and residence in that country to an end. Yet the further graduate work was not in vain; it strengthened credibility and qualifications for employment in other places abroad.

OVERVIEW OF OUR TENTMAKING EXPERIENCE

During the eighteen years we worked abroad in teaching positions, we raised our two children, held jobs in education, maintained a witness to others, and, where we found churches to exist, took advantage of open doors to serve with the body of local believers. Our long-term positions were in Iran, Saudi Arabia, and Hong Kong. Later, under the U.S. State Department, I held a ten-month appointment to Azerbaijan and similar five-month assignments to Qatar and Moldova which were very much part of our tentmaking experience. These three shorter appointments were to give advanced training to local English teachers. Altogether, these six countries of residence abroad represented both highly restricted and unrestricted sites for Christian activity. Even though we were not sent by a missionary agency, wherever we met missionaries in these places, we enjoyed cordial relationships and found ourselves encouraging one another in respect to our different spheres of ministry. Our one and only formal arrangement with a missionary agency was in Iran as field partners with Interserve (then BMMF International). This arrangement, however, was short-lived. After just a few months in the field with that arrangement, the Iranian revolution forced us all to leave. That same agency did not have an ongoing work where we later worked abroad.

Throughout our years in these several countries, one or both of us were employed in fields of education. We fulfilled our responsibilities to our employers and our calling to serve and bear witness to nationals in light of the Great Commission. We used our discretionary hours for friendship evangelism, group Bible study, and hospitality with Christian and non-Christian acquaintances. None of the individuals we befriended had grounds for supposing, and possibly being taken aback with the thought, that we were befriending and sharing our faith to fulfill terms of job requirements. Nor could local Christians suppose that our expectation for them to live out a similar sense of mission in daily life was based on ignorance of the stress and pressures that employed people often face. In fact, we too were merely lay Christians doing what God had called all of us to do wherever we lived and whatever we did for livelihood, only for us in a culture that was not our own. As tentmakers, we were helping local believers to see how local employment and outreach ministry go hand-in-hand as the apostle Paul pointed out to the Christians in Thessalonica: "We did this . . . in order to make ourselves a model for you to follow" (2 Thess 3:9).

LEARNING FROM A NATIONAL BELIEVER

As proponents of lay ministry, we were pleased to learn there were already nationals in some localities for whom lay ministry was not a strange notion. Once, while living in Iran, prior to the Islamic revolution, we encountered a splendid example of a national believer diligently sharing his faith with friends and acquaintances in his own cultural setting. As a lay Christian and our neighbor in Tehran, Brother Misak belonged to the small Armenian minority. He was employed at Iran's Ministry of Finance. After Ann and I had left Tehran and moved to the city of Shiraz far to the South, we got a glimpse of this older brother's scope of personal witness and follow-up ministry when he with wife and two teenage children were our guests for several days during the spring holiday season. By the second day, various long-time contacts of his came to our door, like one young soldier assigned to Shiraz, or rang our phone to arrange a visit. As people came, we watched him seated in a cushioned chair in our living room with a large open Bible and his guests around him as he taught them further from the Scriptures and prayed for them. And these were only some of his many contacts now scattered around the country long before the rise of email, cell phones, and texting. This employed Christ follower presented us with a beautiful picture of what we ourselves wanted to be as tentmakers in that setting. His example reinforced upon us the power of a layperson's witness and its potential to impact friends and acquaintances.

TODAY'S NEED AND OPPORTUNITIES FOR TENTMAKERS

Clearly, today there is huge opportunity and critical need for many thousands of earnest cross-cultural tentmakers, not only for so-called limited access or closed countries, but for all spiritually under-resourced countries and localities throughout the world. There are wide-ranging opportunities for residence and work abroad as the present day's estimated 6,000,000 American citizens now living outside the boundaries of the U.S. indicates. Many of these hold full-time jobs, and some are true followers of Jesus Christ. Few, however, see themselves engaged in spreading the good news of the gospel in the spheres of their vocational calling. Meanwhile, at least one major established missionary society with hundreds of missionaries positioned in dozens of countries recently encountered a serious shortfall in funding for their workers. Tamara Audi, in an article in the *Wall Street Journal*, reported that the long-established Southern Baptist Convention's International Mission Board had found it necessary to retract their commitments and call for missionaries to take early retirement for lack of sufficient denominational funding (*Wall Street Journal*, October

26, 2015). The pullback had been caused by a shortfall in contributions from churches and individuals.

My wife, as a member of the mission board of a large suburban American church that partially supports scores of missionaries, has seen the challenge and cost of the fundraising requirement of traditional missionary candidates. She has seen cases of young missionary candidates spending two years and more traveling around the country in a quest for their needed support—spending more time and funds for raising an elusive sum than what one might spend to obtain a well-chosen master's degree for strategic overseas employment. Another current drawback for some young missionary candidates is a mountain of debt due to college loans. Yet, a tentmaker might not only generate the necessary funds for living and ministering abroad, but also for paying down debts while working abroad much like one might do while working in the homeland. Thus, today there is a multi-faceted rationale for selecting tentmaking as a long-term vehicle for cross-cultural evangelism.

As I reflect on our years abroad as tentmakers and the many kinds of ministries that opened up for us, I see specific areas of God's gracious provision across our careers working abroad. At the outset of our venturing abroad I was not aware of all these areas of God's working for us, but now looking back, that divine activity stands out boldly. I aim to spotlight these areas of God's faithfulness for the benefit of would-be tentmakers as they ponder and plan their own ventures abroad. The following twelve chapters offer insight on specific areas of tentmaking for the guidance and reassurance of anyone contemplating a tentmaking career. My hope is that our discoveries, reflections, and recommendations are of some help to others.

3

Finding Employment Abroad

A WOULD-BE TENTMAKER CAN find appropriate employment in a given field of expertise in a wide range of countries that need Christian witness and discipleship training. Thanks to the internet, a job search nowadays is much different from the slow-moving and often tedious approach of letter writing and long waits for replies. With the internet, one can uncover many possibilities in a short time and cull out from the many the most promising. Inquiries and their replies move along rapidly. Yet, some of the old ways of searching involving personal visits and networking remain highly effective.

Once while searching widely for an overseas position through written applications and postal services, I spotted a job advertisement in the weekly *Chronicle of Higher Education,* a source of news and job openings for university faculty and administrators. The position was in Saudi Arabia. Two weeks after posting my application, I received a phone call to verify my interest in the position, and days later I was invited to go to Houston, TX for an interview. Shortly after returning home from the interview, I was offered a job that I accepted, a position that took me with my family to a remote and fascinating part of the kingdom of Saudi Arabia. Once there, we found ourselves in the cooler, mountainous region of

Finding Employment Abroad

the kingdom that looked down upon the Red Sea far off in the horizon. We were awed by the griffon vultures with their seven-foot wingspan soaring among the mountains and amused by the packs of baboons that scavenged in the nearby city dump. In the city of Abha we joined a host of faculty members and their families, mostly of Arab origin, from surrounding countries to serve a newly developing university with a medical school.

However, during the first two years in that country's highly restricted environment, we longed for a position where there would be more contact with local people and more acceptance of even the smallest Christian expression. What I prayerfully did toward that end was more complex than an internet search, and one that proved to be highly successful. I had learned that a major American airline company was offering round-the-world air tickets with unlimited stops at a reasonable cost. The one condition was that the sequence of stops must keep moving in the same direction, either eastward or westward from the start. So at the end of the academic year for the customary summer trip home given to foreign faculty in Saudi Arabia, I flew westward with my family to the United States with my round-the-world ticket in hand. Three weeks before the summer's end, I left home heading further westward for stops in Tokyo, Hong Kong, Singapore, Jakarta, and Kuala Lumpur. Earlier I had found an educational directory entitled *The World of Learning* from which I had jotted down names and addresses of institutions of higher learning in the cities I planned to visit, institutions that seemed worth checking out for possible employment. I also had names and contact information of a few people I had earlier reached through correspondence or had known previously as a colleague elsewhere.

So at each stop I found my way through a strange airport, out onto the streets, and into a taxi for a ride to a budget hotel. There I spread out a tourist map to get an orientation and plot a course to one or more destinations. Upon reaching the relevant institutional offices, I asked to see a department head or an assistant. In those meetings, I explained my interest in an open position for one year off in the future. This led to a couple of substantive discussions and my handing over a resume to those who expressed interest in keeping in contact. Casual conversation with people already employed as foreigners, or as nationals, in these educational settings was extremely helpful in discerning local worker morale, long-term prospects, housing options, adequacy of salary for living expenses, schooling available for children, and more. I also tried to gain some impression of the relative openness to Christian expression in that community and country.

Months after my return to Saudi Arabia for our third year in that country, I continued to communicate by mail with contacts in the places I had visited. Positions seemed to be opening for me at two of the universities I had visited, one in Kuala Lumpur and the other in Hong Kong. The latter extended an invitation in the spring to visit for a formal interview. How that worked out was another example of God's intervention and the faithfulness of our prayer supporters. At that time, Saudi Arabian authorities procedurally held the passports of foreign faculty members to be sure no one left before the end of the school year for anything other than a personal emergency or death of a close relative. With trepidation I approached my immediate supervisor about the invitation and told him about a possible position where I would not have to pay three months salary up front per year for my children's schooling as I would have to do in Saudi Arabia with the newly announced change of policy. I gained his approval, and he accompanied me to the office of the Saudi Dean of Education. My supervisor did the talking stating the case for my children to have their schooling where it would be more affordable. The dean approved, saw to it that I got my passport, and gave me his blessing, "Have a safe trip to Hong Kong." I made arrangements for my classes to be taught while away, and few colleagues were even aware of my three-day absence. In Hong Kong I interviewed for the headship of a newly formed Language Center at one of the smaller universities, a position with benefits covering the greater portion of the children's schooling. I accepted the position they offered long before an offer from Kuala Lumpur came many months too late to consider.

Finding Employment Abroad

Today's tentmakers benefit from a proliferation of fields of specialization relevant to developing economies. In many fields of study, a master's degree with recent experience is sufficient for at least an entry-level teaching position at a college or university. Of course, tentmakers who are qualified teachers of English language, especially English for academic or special purposes, have an abundance of opportunity. That many institutions of higher education are increasingly offering courses through the English medium is a positive development for teachers of other disciplines as well as teachers of English. For example, an English-speaking teacher of information technology may assume a position in Egypt or Thailand while a teacher of English may find a job in the same university upgrading incoming students' high school English. University salaries in less-developed countries are usually less than what is offered in the West. Some privately-run institutes offer better salaries in these fields along with heavier teaching loads. Yet, many developing or highly developed countries around the globe have good universities and colleges offering promising positions to qualified applicants.

My wife, a certified and experienced elementary school teacher, found stimulating work opportunities in our overseas situations. During our first year in Tehran, before our first child was born, she taught English at a women's college following an established curriculum. Then, when occupied at home with child care, she volunteered as a board member of the newly-formed Christian Henry Martin School in Tehran and later similarly served on the board of the established secular international school in Shiraz. She also tutored special needs children. She once set up and ran a half-day kindergarten where there were employed people of several nationalities who wanted to hire a qualified person to help their children learn English. In Hong Kong she moved from substitute teacher to full-time teacher to deputy head of an English elementary school enrolling children of both Chinese and foreign nationalities.

Teaching is just one of many kinds of employment open to tentmakers. We have met long-term tentmakers in information

Working Abroad with Purpose

technology, business, finance, law, microloans, engineering, medicine, paramedical work, hospital administration, and music. Increasingly, jobs can be expected to appear in environmental studies, ecology, marine biology, water purification, waste management, and agriculture as well as in food processing and nutrition. Library science is a highly relevant field. A friend in India is finding increasing opportunity to use her training as a nurse to help pioneer an area of public health. Undoubtedly, with the advance of technology and the successive levels of development in emerging countries, the specific professional skills in most demand are ever-shifting. My own skill set and qualifications, which served me so well for many years, may not for long be as marketable since many nationals are obtaining similar qualifications. The upcoming generation of tentmakers, when facing educational opportunities and choices, can research and discover the fields of study that best match the needs of the envisioned country or region.

Tentmakers might gain inspiration and encouragement from what I witnessed in recent short-term work among refugees in Turkey. One earns his keep through taming expensive birds for sale in Istanbul's many bird stores. He takes one bird at a time to his humble living quarters and trains it over several days to be calm when held, not to flutter and bite the fingers or nose of a handler. Another who is skilled in Persian carpet repair was making a living by collecting damaged or tattered carpets from shops in the bazaar to repair at his small apartment before returning them for an agreed price. The tentmaker, of course, does not enter and reside as a refugee, but rather comes with credentials for formal employment. However, these industrious refugees demonstrate the rewards of ingenuity, creativity, and perseverance in establishing a means of income.

Decades ago, before the appearance of the internet, Global Opportunities, the precursor to Global Intent, a service organization for tentmakers, laboriously gleaned job openings from journals and newsletters in numerous professional fields worldwide to establish a job bank for would-be tentmakers. Now, job seekers can ably search the websites relevant to their own professional field

Finding Employment Abroad

for information on jobs. Also, universities in the West commonly offer placement services to their own graduates, a possible source of jobs abroad. Personal contact with donor-supported missionaries is a potential source of leads for employment. The home offices of missionary agencies may be a source of information on overseas ministry opportunities, but home office personnel of mission agencies may be unfamiliar with the tentmaking model or hold reservations about it. They may rather offer suggestions to work within the framework of their own ongoing donor-supported ministries. However, a few missionary agencies have formulated policy for a working relationship with tentmakers. Undoubtedly, a helpful source of jobs in a particular overseas setting is any known tentmaker already in the region where the tentmaker aspires to take up residence.

Our own means of obtaining employment abroad in fields of education sometimes entailed methodical investigation and other times simply fortuitous developments, but sooner or later we would see that our employment was God's provision for us and an answer to our supporters' prayers. Among the unplanned and fortuitous openings was the timely teaching position at Tehran University negotiated by the University of Illinois. In Hong Kong it was the sudden opening of a teaching position at an international elementary school and the eventual administrative position for Ann. Other illustrations are an unofficial kindergarten opening in a city of the Middle East followed by a surprising opportunity to teach English to the young daughters of the provincial deputy governor. Some positions came by deliberate search, such as the round-the-world trip with many stops. Equally of God's provision for us were teaching positions in U.S. universities after the forced departure from Iran due to the revolution in 1978, and again when we decided to return to long-term employment in our homeland in 1993.

SOME ONGOING SHORT-TERM POSSIBILITIES

One option for American citizens for short-term work abroad in a wide range of capacities is the Peace Corps program of the U.S. Department of State. Peace Corps volunteers are given three months of training in language, culture, and practicalities and then assigned to one of over sixty countries. Two-year appointments are to Africa, Central Asia, Southeast Asia, Central and South America, and Mexico. Peace Corps volunteers work in the fields of education, business, information technology, agriculture, health, and community development. Volunteers receive a stipend enabling them to live on a standard similar to that of the people they serve. Their medical and dental needs are covered, and upon completion of two years of service they receive a bonus to help in their transition. Completion of a Peace Corps assignment adds significantly to a person's resume for subsequent longer-term employment elsewhere.

In the Peace Corps, a volunteer represents the best of American values in addressing an area of basic need of a particular group of people. As a Christian, the volunteer keeps Jesus Christ in view as a model of compassionate care of others. At the same time, the volunteer is ready to discreetly respond to questions and comments about his/her lifestyle and faith. A volunteer's replies can lead to life-impacting exchanges. A volunteer is always free to discuss matters of personal faith with peers, be they compatriots or nationals, both on the job or after hours. A two-year term of work of this kind with practical support and accountability often proves to be a valuable learning experience for one's ongoing tentmaking career. It also helps to discover how God provides for fellowship, spiritual nurture, and avenues of Christian witness. In one town in Central Asia, where I was giving workshops for local English teachers, I met a Christian Peace Corps volunteer who had been meeting often with two other like-minded volunteers for prayer together. In another country, I met a Christian worker who spoke of coming to faith in Christ while serving as a Peace Corps worker through the witness of another worker.

Finding Employment Abroad

Another option for a similar cross-cultural experience is to pursue a degree in a foreign university that uses English as a medium of instruction. This, however, would involve a measure of self-support as most students from other countries do not usually qualify for local grants. The cost of tuition and living accommodations, however, is often far less than the cost of tuition, boarding, and daily living in Western countries. For example, in Shiraz, Iran, we had fellowship with a British citizen who was pursuing a master's degree in engineering at the local university. His research on the recycling potential of the city's trash was of much interest to the city's authorities and elsewhere in Iran. He went on to spend many years working in his field in other countries. Many foreign universities have functioning student Christian fellowships. For examples, the website of the International Fellowship of Evangelical Students (IFES) states the IFES network now extents to over one hundred and sixty countries. A campus Christian fellowship can provide opportunities for both fellowship and joint activity in evangelism.

4

Obtaining Prayer Support

TENTMAKERS NEED SUSTAINED PRAYER support throughout their time abroad just as donor-supported workers do. Some have maintained that unless a church establishes financial ties with Christian workers, commitment to pray for them soon falters. Patrick Lai contends, "Churches pray for those they pay."[1] He further suggests Christian workers who do not need financial support should at least request a token amount of support to ensure that the church prays. Hopefully, churches do pray for those they financially support, but we never felt that people forgot to support us in prayer simply because we were not asking for their donations and were earning what we needed for living and serving abroad. We believe our prayer supporters were diligent in prayer as long as we kept them informed. I doubt the church in first-century Antioch that released Saul and Barnabas for ministry elsewhere prayed less for them because they did not have need or means to give then sustained financial support.

Before going abroad for the first time, my wife and I wanted to first secure a small core of prayer partners who would pray for us daily, especially during our initial year of settling into an unfamiliar culture, new living situation, and new workplace. We

1. Lai, *Tentmaking*, 60.

Obtaining Prayer Support

needed prayer for God's leading to meet people with minds open to the gospel and for daily wisdom in all our decisions. We needed intercessors who would faithfully turn our written updates into earnest prayer. There were sure to be challenges, disappointments, and obstacles. Prayer supporters for us meant people who would not merely read about our intriguing experiences at that time, in a relatively unknown part of the world, but people who would pray for us systematically. So, we asked God to give us at least ten or twelve couples or individuals who would pray daily as well as others who would pray often in some fashion. That small core of daily prayer supporters eventually consisted of some family members, a few couples from a small fellowship group, and other friends who had known us for years. With this core of prayer supporters, the commitment was mutual. I recall times while standing or seated in a slow-moving, crowded Tehran bus on the way to the university, mentally going through the names of those supporters making brief prayers for each. Of course, there were other individuals and church members totaling more than a hundred who asked to be kept informed, and we valued their interest and prayers for us as well.

Once the needed prayer support was secured, we found a way of keeping supporters abreast of our activities in some detail at least a few times per year. At the beginning, our means of communicating with these partners was primitive by today's standards, but advanced in comparison with early missionaries from the West to Asia, like Henry Martyn, who had to wait up to a year for an answer after he posted a letter to home. We didn't have easy access to telephone service during our first two years abroad. We knew of no mechanism for sending monthly detailed reports to a hundred or more contacts with the mere touch of a button on a keypad. Instead, we relied upon the old blue single-sheet aerogrammes that took a week or two to reach our core supporters. We found ways to get detailed news and requests to all the others at least twice a year. When the flow of information was limited, we were fully satisfied if people were praying for us along the lines of the apostle Paul's prayers for the believers in Ephesus and Philippi—that we would increase in the knowledge of God, make wise choices, and learn how daily to sense and do the Lord's will.

In general, since most would-be tentmakers are unlikely to have been vetted and approved by a missionary agency, they are apt to face some questioning when approaching a church missionary committee for systematic prayer support. There may be questions about the applicant's qualifications, overall preparedness, strength of purpose, and lines of accountability in the projected overseas ministry. Certainly, the desired prayer support will come most easily when approaching church leaders where the tentmaker had been known to be a faithful church member with an outreach vision. A tentmaker's home church, the church regularly attended during university days, and any church attended as a working professional certainly would be inclined to specify an occasion for interested church members to learn of the envisioned ministry. Assuring a missionary committee there will be no call for funding may make it easier to get scheduled for a presentation at a church gathering. Aside from churches, individuals that the would-be tentmaker has partnered with in church or parachurch ministries in the past may wish to be counted among the prayer supporters.

My wife and I found that those with whom we had had intimate Christian fellowship were the most ready to promise their support. Our home churches had known us for several years or more as people committed to outreach ministry. To our knowledge, there was no puzzlement over our ending the donor support we had received during our years of InterVarsity campus ministry to pursue a year of university study in preparation for employment abroad. They understood that the study would lead to employment and a footing for personal outreach abroad. Our vision made sense to them. I recall my home church pastor, once a missionary himself, saying something to the effect, "We know wherever you go you will get involved in outreach to others, so you can count on our support." Those who promised to pray for us and our ministry in Iran continued their support when the national revolution forced us to return home and figure out our next steps. Years later, when we were resettled in Saudi Arabia and later in Hong Kong,

Obtaining Prayer Support

many of the same supporters still wished to receive our updates for their prayer support.

In many respects, our two home churches viewed us as two of the many missionaries they supported financially and through prayer. I do not recall any church commissioning us for service abroad, but we had opportunities to speak at church gatherings shortly before our departures. Looking back, I think we would have done well to ask our churches for a formal commissioning at a church service. Nevertheless, our prayer supporters were heartily behind us and many sought extra updates from our parents. I vividly recall members of my home church, including my newly widowed mother, crowded together at a receiving gate at Detroit's Metro Airport to welcome us home for the summer after our first two years abroad. For my mother, it was a time to take into her arms her first grandchild only weeks after the death of my father.

5

Securing Visas and Permits

A TENTMAKER WHO HAS secured employment in the target country prior to entry is well-positioned to receive the required entry visa and permits for long-term residence and work. This is in contrast to Christian workers who attempt to reside in a limited-access country on the basis of a tourist visa with periodic renewals, usually by means of exiting and reentering the country every six months or less. Recently, a donor-supported friend who is having a remarkable long-term ministry in a Western Asian country applied for another short-term visa renewal. The friendly immigration officer handling his application commented with something like, "We like you and think you're a good guy. I can pass your application on to my superiors, but they might raise some questions—you, here, as a tourist for thirteen years?" So, my friend, awaiting the outcome of his renewal application, asked teammates for earnest prayer that the visa renewal process would once again go forward without a hitch. For a tentmaker, the process is less intimidating. In my own situation as a contracted employee of an institution within the country, I experienced no anxiety over an initial visa and related permits I and my family needed. In fact, none of the countries where I found employment entailed worries about an entry visa. Neither were renewals a nail-biting

Securing Visas and Permits

experience. Visas seemed to be granted and renewed by virtue of the job I was given in that country addressing some recognized national priority.

As foreign lands gained independence in the decades following World War II, after years of colonization or maneuvering by Western powers, the ease of access for missionaries changed. Missionaries were increasingly perceived as agents of imperialism, a challenge to the majority religion, and therefore not so welcome. In more recent years, many countries have adopted an economic-based protectionism, a rejection of Western values, and a discriminating religious bias. Some have even chosen a pronounced anti-American stance. This is less apt to be the case with Christian workers coming from the Far East or other regions. For workers from Western nations, these perceptions slowed down or halted the granting of entry visas and residence permits. Foreigners as religious workers are easily viewed as people advancing mainly alien interests. However, a foreigner who accepts a job in an economic or educational sector that the government deems an under-resourced priority is likely to be treated more favorably. In general, applicants qualified to meet a recognized national need and advance local interests are more likely to get the desired authorizations.

In our own experience, after settling for an advertised position while outside the target country, we followed the new employer's instructions on making application for entry and work permits and simply waited while the bureaucratic wheels turned. Delays sometimes occurred due to slow-moving background checks and approvals or simply by bureaucratic inefficiencies. On one occasion, after I had negotiated with employers in two different countries and had settled on the one, the other was still working on my application long after I was involved in a new job elsewhere, in spite of my informing them I was no longer available. All in all, in due time we always received the necessary permission for entry, residence, and work in the countries where we had secured employment. We never had to exit a country in order to renew our visas.

Working Abroad with Purpose

Once we were settled and working in an overseas setting, most renewals were handled by service personnel of the employing institution. The process may be different when aiming to enter a country to set up one's own business—something I have never considered doing. (See Patrick Lai's *Business for Transformation* for detailed help on such ventures.) If a person enters a target country on a tourist visa in order to search for a job, or if one changes jobs within a country after living and working there, the process could be more drawn out (as I learned in Iran where I twice changed employers). The tentmaker who enters the target country as an employee of an international firm, or a government department working in that overseas context, can usually expect the employing institution to handle the steps of securing the necessary clearances and permits.

In those regions where I held long-term university teaching positions—the Middle East, Central Asia, and the Far East—and the three countries where I had shorter U.S. State Department appointments, my experience in gaining entry was the same. My family and I never experienced anxiety over this matter. Our places of employment ranged from those often referred to as closed or "limited access" to those more easily accessed like, at the time, British-run Hong Kong. In all cases, our ease of entry was undoubtedly related to the host countries' need for the skills we represented and the unambiguous role we were to fill. Each time, upon arriving in those different international airports for the first time, it was the employer or his representative who greeted my family and me and transported us to our initial residence or temporary quarters—except in our initial entry into Iran. That was because we entered the country by overland travel from Turkey. In that case, it was rather a tentmaker friend who met us at the Tehran bus station, and after he and his wife accommodated us for a few nights at their home, he helped me find the office of my employer.

6

Settling on Housing and Schooling

REFLECTIONS ON OUR PAST ARRANGEMENTS

HOUSING IS A HUGE factor in the life of a tentmaker, a factor that can facilitate the envisioned ministry or hamper it. Housing, like the workplace, can be an avenue of natural contact with the common people in the host country. A tentmaker, once in the target country, aims for housing that satisfies personal needs, family life, and home-based ministry. If one's work contract contains no mention of housing or assistance in obtaining it beyond a possible reference to a housing allowance, the tentmaker will usually have to find housing on the open market. Any help or informed advice from the employer, experienced fellow employees, or other Christian workers in the community can be extremely helpful. A search for housing can be, as we learned, an instructive but sometimes challenging introduction to the local culture.

To generalize about finding housing on one's own, beyond whatever tips or help the employer may give, a tentmaker can explain to a local rental agent just what is expected in the way of housing. The agent's response will either confirm what the new employer or colleagues may have suggested about terms of rental service and the probable cost of housing or lead to a process of negotiation and adjustment. One soon learns how firm asking rental costs are and how much room there is for bargaining. In time, the tentmaker will also learn just how binding or flexible a given rental contract will prove to be. Before signing a rental contract, the client can test the waters to find out what he or she can expect or demand in respect to the property's need for cleaning, repainting, appliances, or utilities. Most employers would provide some help in checking the details of a proposed lease in the local language before the signing. Indeed, finding one's housing in the local market provides lessons on how many things are done in that culture, valuable insight for a long-term resident.

A broad search for housing not only reveals local practices in the housing market but helps one understand traditional values, particularly as reflected in older dwellings—the configuration and size of rooms, provisions for security, attitudes toward privacy, and arrangements for heating, cooking, and washing. When hunting for housing for my family of four in the more remote city of Kerman, Iran—a city of 40,000—I was shown homes built two or more generations in the past. I saw one home where the kitchen sink counters were only a bit above knee level and homes in which a sit-down Western toilet would have been an anomaly for most older local residents. The home we settled upon had a private walled-in yard but an odd configuration of rooms. For our desired third bedroom, we had to settle for a small room set on the roof accessible by an internal stairway, a room likely designed for a live-in household maid.

Earlier in Shiraz, Iran, we had negotiated and settled for a two-storied house with a walled-in yard and a garden featuring rose bushes and mint. The land phone that came with the house was the envy of our few foreign friends in the same city. We felt secure with a signed official two-year lease. But shortly after the first year, our elderly landlord sent his household helper on his bicycle from another part of town to ask access to the home in order to measure all the windows. Ann surmised immediately what was unfolding. The measuring was no doubt for real curtains, but the visit was also a message that we should begin looking for

Settling on Housing and Schooling

some other dwelling. We learned later that the owner's son and wife were returning from America and were promised our living quarters. Eventually we were officially notified to vacate. Yet, did we not have a two-year lease? We were perplexed and did our best to stall. But good local friends advised us that it would be in our own best interests to move. God provided another place for us, a single-level apartment with a walled-in yard in the center of town. Soon we were comfortably resettled and again hosting friends and contacts as usual.

We found that each housing situation we had for any length of time brought unanticipated benefits. Our first place of residence abroad was in an apartment that was a two-minute walk from the residence of an American couple who had been in Iran for many years as tentmakers. We had once heard of them and were surprised to discover they were our own neighbors. Our second home in Tehran featured our accommodating landlord living on the level immediately below us with three daughters who thrilled in entertaining our one-year-old daughter by the hour. The first home we had in Shiraz put us strategically on a side street in a row of adjacent homes occupied by local university faculty members and their families. In Saudi Arabia we had an apartment in a fifteen-storied apartment building in the center of town where faculty members, mostly from Arab countries, lived with their families. We were all in close proximity to one another for easy social engagement. During our first week in that high-rise, a Palestinian physics professor with wife and children reached out to us in practical friendship transporting us to stores far and near to stock up our kitchen shelves. Before long, we ourselves had hosted at least twenty fellow faculty members from the West Bank, Lebanon, Libya, Afghanistan, Egypt, and elsewhere. As for our apartment in Hong Kong, we discovered we were in the same apartment block where one of Hong Kong's best-known entertainers humbly lived with his wife and two sons. Our own son not only palled around with those two boys, but was sometimes taken along on their upscale family vacations outside of Hong Kong.

It may make for an easier transition to new surroundings to be placed in a fully furnished apartment or villa in a westernized, expatriate, gated compound, as is often the case for people contracted with a large multinational corporation or government agency. For such employees, the cost of housing and furnishing may even be fully covered by the employer. Housing of this kind may be very appealing. A unit with a fenced-in yard with garden, provisions for children's schooling and recreation, even a shared or private swimming pool, is not exceptional for a well-qualified foreign employee. In such a compound, residents are likely to be from several Western countries if not all from the employee's own homeland. Tentmakers with this kind of expatriate housing, however, may count it a serious drawback if they discover their living situation is far removed from the local citizens. At the same time, they are apt to face strong social pressure to spend their free time in many expatriate activities which are not easily dismissed time after time. If the workplace similarly involves few nationals, the new employee may find that natural contact with local people is severely limited.

In my years working abroad in positions of higher education, on three occasions I was assigned to specific living quarters, although in our Hong Kong situation I learned after initially settling in that I was eligible for a housing allowance and free to choose housing on the open market. In that case, after two months we moved from the initial compact, three-bedroom apartment high up in a forty-storied apartment building, where the noise level from cars, trucks, and emergency vehicles below was a constant annoyance. From our living room window, Ann had counted nineteen lanes of traffic moving along or crisscrossing below in a network of highways and overpasses. On the open market we chose a spacious second-floor three-bedroom unit where there was much less noise and more room for guests. Once we absorbed the fact that as new tenants we had to purchase and install three new hot-water heaters for the two bathrooms and the kitchen, we lived there contentedly for nearly eight years. During the first two years the housing allowance was a bit short, but it gradually caught

Settling on Housing and Schooling

up and reached our actual rental expenses. As for needed furnishing, we gradually learned the tricks of closed bidding at auctions on second-hand furniture that once belonged to U.S. diplomatic staff arranged by the American consulate. After several days, items went to the highest bidder and waited for pickup. Piece by piece our home became comfortably furnished.

On two other occasions we found the assigned housing acceptable, one for a three-year residence and the other for a five-month assignment. The first of these was in Abha, Saudi Arabia for our family of four. Upon arrival we were first taken to a "guest house," which we found in questionable readiness. We wondered if the sheets had been changed and how far we might be from a place to buy something to put in the refrigerator. After a couple of nights, we were transported to a high-rise apartment suited to our needs except for the lack of separate bedrooms for our two children, a brother and sister. We managed by creative partitioning of the one bedroom into two sections by the placement of two six-foot tall portable wardrobes. The other assigned housing was for a five-month Sabbatical-leave semester in Qatar at a time when Ann was unable to accompany me. I was immediately taken from the airport to the eight-room upscale villa, where I lived comfortably using just the sitting room, a bedroom, and kitchen. Within walking distance was a huge Carrefour supermarket with twenty checkout lanes. Ann was able to join me in this large villa for just two weeks due to her administrative duties back home.

In Iran we were never assigned housing or given a specific housing allowance. Upon our initial entry, we benefited greatly from the help of another tentmaker who had spoken for us to take an apartment newly vacated by a departing missionary couple. In subsequent years in Iran, we had to fend for housing ourselves on the open market with the help of rental agents. Both apartments we had in Tehran served us well, and we had cordial relationships with the landlords. It was in Shiraz that the landlord broke the rental agreement after the first year requiring us to search for another place. Later, when we returned to Iran after three years of graduate studies, we again worked with agents for housing in the smaller city of Kerman.

I have no regrets about the various housing arrangements we settled for. We never lived in a closed expatriate community that required visitors to show their identity papers and declare their purpose in order to get past security guards. In all our living situations, friends could visit us, announced or unannounced, needing to do nothing more than ring a doorbell and tell us who they were on the built-in microphone. Furthermore, we were usually within walking distance of fruit and vegetable stands, small shops of many kinds, or even an uncovered bazaar with rows and rows of foodstuffs and merchandise. For us, these housing arrangements aligned well with our purpose for going abroad, especially entertaining local friends for coffee, meals, and Bible study. And while they were still with us, these places served the interests of our children as well.

SCHOOLING FOR CHILDREN

Along with the search for adequate housing, tentmaking couples with school-age children must consider what options are available for their children's schooling unless they do homeschooling. The local options for all expatriates, be they tentmakers, donor-supported missionaries, business people, or diplomatic personnel depend greatly upon the number of foreign families living in the same community. Tentmakers employed by large international firms or departments of government are most apt to have much or all of the children's education provided for—in one way or another—by the terms of employment. Those who have to arrange for that schooling on their own must determine their best affordable option. The fees at most international schools are out of reach for many tentmakers. Some tentmakers may find they have access to a local Christian school established primarily for missionary children where tuition is more affordable. Should either the husband or wife be a qualified teacher, the option of a teaching job at a missionary school, with or without salary, could entail discounted

Settling on Housing and Schooling

tuition or even a complete tuition waver for one or more children. Some even opt to have their children enter good, local, public schools at little or no expense. The local language is an initial challenge, but young children learn the local language remarkably fast. Distance learning online is sure to be an increasing option along with homeschooling and the wide variety of curricula that option now offers.

As mentioned above, our own children had access to schooling, paid in part by the employer, at an international school on a military compound in our remote part of Saudi Arabia, serving primarily children of foreign employees. In Hong Kong, they both had critical years of schooling in the British School system attended by children of both foreign employees and children of local Chinese families who preferred an English education. We arranged for our daughter to have her final year of secondary education at a missionary school in Taiwan, an hour's flight from us in Hong Kong. That school's American curriculum and her living away from home helped make for a smoother transition to an American university the following year. In general, families living abroad send their children to their homeland for any desired postsecondary education.

7

Discovering Fellowship in the Host Country

ONCE IN THE TARGET country, tentmakers can usually find others of like mind for meaningful fellowship even where no organized churches exist. To illustrate, shortly after settling into our apartment in Saudi Arabia, we received a letter from a prayer supporter in the U.S. giving us the name of a Christian medical doctor serving at a military hospital thirty miles from our town. We reached this person by phone and learned his term of service was just for one month. But he spoke of a newly arrived long-term American medical doctor with wife and four children who had recently come to his own expatriate community. We had them over to our home for dinner within a week, and two days later, the new family visited us again for fellowship on a Friday, the equivalent of the Western Sunday as in much of the Arab world. After a few more weeks and our purchase of a second-hand car, we began driving to the other city on Fridays to join others for a home meeting of singing, Bible study, and prayer within their expatriate compound. We also had some special activities for the children. Those weekly gatherings with up to a dozen adult believers of several nationalities were our only occasions of corporate fellowship during our three years in Saudi Arabia. To our knowledge, other than ourselves, there

Discovering Fellowship in the Host Country

seldom were more than one or two other practicing Christians in our own city, people who appeared to have an authentic Christian experience.

Wherever we lived abroad, except in Saudi Arabia, we discovered an expatriate church or a welcoming local church, or both. In Tehran, for our own nurture we attended the Tehran Bible Church where missionaries, foreign workers, and even a few local Iranians worshipped and mingled together. Many participants could preach or teach so there was no need at the time for a salaried pastor. In Shiraz, at the centrally located Anglican church, with an intricately designed Persian dome, we participated in the services for a small group of expatriates on Fridays, the weekly holiday, and the larger gathering of Iranians in Farsi on Sunday evenings after work hours. In both Qatar and Azerbaijan, there were growing expatriate churches.

In less restricted contexts, there were many established churches to choose from. In Hong Kong, churches conducting services in English represented a variety of traditions and denominations along with scores of small Chinese churches using the local Cantonese dialect. As a family, we first attended the evangelical St. Andrews Anglican Church where we found friendship with believers from the United Kingdom, Australia, New Zealand, and European countries. We later joined other Americans in the founding of a new church called the Evangelical Community Church that attracted both expatriates and local English-speaking Chinese, many of whom had attended universities in America or the United Kingdom. That church has since developed into two large congregations.

In Moldova we were welcomed into the newly founded Russian language Agape Church with its own new building and a surprising number of attending young people who were new in the faith. We were warmly embraced by the founding pastor's two sons who had graduated from a Christian college in the United States. We sat through many Russian language services, sometimes getting the gist of sermons through the help of young friends who sat with us putting their English learning to good use. Some young folks who were new believers welcomed our sharing and counsel on the challenges they were facing. Making this our place of worship on Sundays gave opportunity to occasionally preach with one of the pastor's sons serving as translator.

In all our places of residence abroad, without having formal ties with a missionary agency, we habitually searched for like-minded believers, expatriate or local. God was faithful in meeting our need for fellowship. Over time, we found ourselves meeting with believers of other nationalities, different church traditions, and of different callings and outlooks. Many of our friends were from other countries, residing abroad in different capacities, and many were local citizens who were genuine followers of Jesus Christ. In countries where missionaries could reside and carry on formal ministries, donor-supported missionaries were among our friends, some newly arrived like ourselves, and others well-established in the local culture. Some of these with different backgrounds gathered together with us regularly for sharing, prayer, and mutual encouragement. These relationships enlarged our appreciation of the body of Christ. In Iran, we were encouraged by Pentecostal friends. In Saudi Arabia, we came to admire an openly Christian Coptic couple and the faith of believers from India and Ghana. In Hong Kong, Chinese believers, some converted to Christ locally and others during student days abroad, became our special friends. We grew to appreciate so very much people of like faith from England, Scotland, Norway, Singapore, and Australia.

While these kinds of relationships were in play in most places we lived, the most dramatic blending together of like-minded believers, quite apart from any advanced planning, occurred in Shiraz, Iran. This was at a time when entry for traditional missionaries was facing some restrictions. One of the foremost magnets drawing tentmaker-oriented workers to the city was the local university where English was widely used for instruction. During our first year in the city, we had fellowship with an American chemistry professor and family, a Canadian mathematician and family, and a physics instructor and family from the Netherlands. A year later, a Scottish radiographer joined the fellowship. Also with us

Discovering Fellowship in the Host Country

was a British Christian graduate student working locally on a master's degree. A few donor-supported Christian workers joined this outreach-oriented circle. As a group of seven or eight men, we met at one of our homes weekly for breakfast, prayer, accountability, and the planning of an occasional outreach effort. This was a team assembled by God for mutual encouragement and the planting of the seed of the gospel in some hard and resistant soil. This experience helped us learn that wherever God might lead us to serve, he would provide the fellowship and team experience we needed. God's hand was not only guiding our own movements as tentmakers, but also the steps of others who were similarly following God's leading to distant places.

8

Seeing Opportunities for Outreach

WHILE A TENTMAKER PLANS for his or her positioning in a specific workplace abroad, the many new acquaintances to be made in that new setting are a matter of God's sovereign placement. The people in that particular work situation are not there by chance. God's plan for the individuals in that context is unfolding so that some are in a place where they will encounter the good news of the Christian gospel. God is also at work in their inner lives. The Scriptures make clear that God the Holy Spirit is at work convincing people of "guilt in regard to sin and righteousness and judgment" (John 16:8). That promise assures a tentmaker that among those many new acquaintances in the new situation will be some at a stage of preparation to appreciate thoughts drawn from the Christian Scriptures and a spoken witness to the truth. Some consciously, or subconsciously, are seeking answers to the big questions about life's purpose and meaning in the face of the many dubious or unconvincing claims they have encountered elsewhere. The tentmaker takes up his/her new position with that conviction and confidence.

For most tentmakers, the work situation is the most assured circle of sustained contact and friendship with nationals. In his major volume on BAM, Johnson shared what he understood to be a common stereotype of a tentmaker, that is, a person who is "earning money in one place, so that . . . [he/she] . . . can minister in another"[1] This was not Johnson's own conception of a tentmaker, and certainly it is not what I mean by a tentmaker. People holding that stereotype fail to grasp one of the greatest assets of tentmaking, namely, daily contact with fellow employees, nationals who are usually ignorant or misinformed of the Christian gospel. Further, tentmakers are not like the many employees in America who are eager for a job enabling them to work from the comfort of home. Rather, the tentmaker sees a job as a means of personal contact with a range of people as well as a means of livelihood. In the overseas context, the job plots him/her among nationals whom God has put in and around that same workplace to learn in time something of the gospel.

In addition to workplace contacts, there are neighbors, language tutors, local proprietors or traveling vendors, and other service people to meet and show kindness. Of course, in many contexts, the tentmaker's developing proficiency in the local language is a critical enabling factor to capitalize on these many potential relationships. All in all, there is little chance of a tentmaker ending up in an isolated cocoon at home or elsewhere for any length of time. A local job takes him/her out the door and into the surrounding society every workday of the week.

A tentmaker will also encounter opportunities to share the good news of Jesus Christ with people unrelated to the job situation. Tentmaker advocate Ginter points out that life for a Christian entails three types of ministry: vocational, intentional, and serendipitous.[2] By "serendipitous," he is referring to the unplanned, spontaneous, even inconvenient opportunities that unfold in the course of residing and working in a community. To illustrate from our own experience, after my wife and I had formally retired, we were looking forward to further work abroad when I received a U.S. Government-sponsored, five-month teacher training assignment in Moldova, the poorest of the former European Soviet republics. Days before our departure, I was contacted by an

---

1. Johnson, *Business as Mission*, 115.
2. Ginter, "Overcoming Resistance," 210.

American woman, unknown to me, asking if I would hand deliver a small gift package to a certain young man in the country's capital city. She had recently been in Moldova and had struck up some kind of friendship with this Moldovan fellow. A few days later we received her posted package with the necessary information for meeting Sergai, her friend. Having checked the package for safe contents, once we were settled in the city of Chisinau, I reached Sergai by phone and told him where to come for his package. Soon afterward, we met at our apartment and got acquainted. I saw he had a surprisingly good command of English in a country where that would not be expected. We made plans to meet again.

A week later, Sergai and I went for a long walk circling a lake in our part of the city. I learned he was single, a holder of a master's degree in languages, and a nationally ranked chess player, but quite ignorant of the Christian gospel. Before we parted, I passed on to him an English New Testament and suggested where to begin reading. Three months went by while Sergai was away in surrounding countries for chess tournaments as both player and coach. He finally returned to Chisinau from Ukraine and told me that while away he had contracted pneumonia and complications leading to a long hospitalization. However, while confined to bed rest, he began reading that New Testament. After a few more visits together with pointed discussion about the saving work of Jesus and our need for salvation, he was clearly developing an awareness of his own spiritual need. At the end of my fifth month in Moldova, just four days before our planned departure, Sergai stopped by for the last time. After some small talk I asked him how his reading of the Gospels had come along. While staring off into the distance, he paused and asked aloud, "Why did they kill him? Why did they kill him?" With hardly hesitation he himself answered, "He did it for me. I'm a sinner." Suddenly he broke down in tears. We shared further and prayed. Sergai made a genuine commitment to Jesus as his personal Savior and Lord, just days before my wife and I had to bid him farewell.

Over the following four years, Sergai and I had a few brief email exchanges while he seemed always to be on the move. I then decided to make a personal return visit to Moldova to see some of my former teacher trainees and a few other friends, including Sergai. I learned he had been living in Ukraine. For several days I felt my timing was unfortunate since he seemed to be having trouble getting back to Chisinau. Yet, on the last full day of my short stay in Moldova, Sergai arrived in town by means of a twenty-hour bus ride from Ukraine. We met, walked, and talked for hours about the past four years and his spiritual journey. He insisted on paying for the meal we had at a fine restaurant. I was encouraged to hear him recall his commitment to Christ four years earlier and show a new acquaintance with the Scriptures. When we later sat down on a bench in a public park to share further, he asked that he be first to pray. It was a joy to witness this amazing work of God beginning with the delivery of a small gift packet four years earlier, even before my work at the teachers' college had begun.

Yet God had other opportunities as well for my wife and me during the five-month assignment in Moldova. I had the privilege of preaching with translation many times at the Russian evangelical church attended by many young people, and to preach a few times at a Salvation Army weekly gathering. There were young men in the Russian church who were eager to meet up for sharing, Bible discussion, and prayer. Among the trainees at the teachers' college was one who opened up for many long discussions about faith in Jesus Christ, a young woman with whom I later co-published a professional journal article, and whom we arranged a few years later to host in our own home in America when she was in the United States on a Fulbright grant. While residing in Chisinau, my wife and I weekly hosted a group of local English teachers at our apartment for guided discussions, some relating to matters of personal faith. Ann also had personal times with both Moldovan women and professional women from other countries then residing in Moldova.

In the several countries where we lived and were locally employed, we witnessed how friendship with colleagues and others developed naturally. Over time, we entertained scores of non-Christian co-workers, university students, and acquaintances often for meals around our dinner table. Saying grace at mealtime signaled something of our faith—causing one secularized European colleague to snicker at the practice. It was his Norwegian wife whom Ann later led to faith in Jesus Christ. Entertaining was especially easy in the Middle East and Central Asia, where an open home is a deep-seated cultural value. Ann's gift of hospitality, my ongoing encounters with new people at my workplace, and our children's ready response to the attention and warmth of visitors all strengthened our ties with local people.

At the same time, we were recipients of other people's friendship initiatives. Especially in the first confusing days in a new community, one neighbor welcomed us at our door with a bouquet of flowers, another hosted us for tea, others assisted us in grocery shopping, and some plied us with earnest questions about opportunities for study or work in our own home country. Just being there and being engaged in a workplace and community provided more opportunities for personal friendship and witness to Christ than we could fully pursue. A tentmaker, of course, must establish priorities in ministry in light of time and energy constraints, to be discussed later. Surrounded by so many opportunities, only on rare occasions in moments of fleeting doubt did we stop and wonder why it was that God had led us to live and work abroad in this fashion.

In four of the six countries where we lived I had opportunities to preach in established churches. In Saudi Arabia, where churches did not formally exist, several of us men rotated sharing from Scripture in Friday gatherings in a home in a compound for westerners. In Azerbaijan, I taught a small multinational class on Sundays at an expatriate church. In all six countries there were numerous occasions for small group and one-on-one Bible study. Ann had Bible study with individual women in Saudi Arabia and Hong Kong that led to individuals' saving faith. In Hong Kong, a primary means of evangelistic outreach was an office Bible study with colleagues. One such study lead to perhaps the most dramatic conversion we witnessed in our years abroad, that is, the commitment to Christ by a woman who had already established herself

Seeing Opportunities for Outreach

as one of Hong Kong's leading poets. Her open profession of faith and diligent outreach to others through Cantonese and Mandarin led other Chinese to saving faith in Christ including college students and her own husband. In fact, on a return trip to Hong Kong many years later, I learned she was just then being honored at a special ceremony as Hong Kong's most outstanding writer of the previous five years. In retrospect, employment as a tentmaker not only allowed access and witness to colleagues in the workplace, but opened doors to outreach on many fronts.

Beyond what we had planned and hoped for, God often showed us how he is a God of surprises. A major in the Saudi Arabian military once discreetly asked for an Arabic New Testament, a banned book in that country. In one Middle Eastern country, Ann found herself regularly chauffeured to a local upscale residence as an English tutor of two young princesses, daughters of the province's deputy governor. I discovered that my own Western colleagues in a Middle Eastern university, living abroad in single-status capacity, for lack of any familiar entertainment, welcomed participating in a weekly home Bible study of the Gospel of Mark that continued on into a second year with other parts of the Bible. Acquaintance with some Arab professors in that university led to long-term friendships in some cases, so that years later, in other contexts, we met again and could pursue deeper discussion of the Christian gospel.

One example of reconnecting years later occurred seventeen years after our leaving Saudi Arabia. I was just weeks into a five-month Fulbright assignment to give further training to English teachers in Qatar when I met up with the Iraqi biology professor who had previously lived with his family in our apartment complex in Saudi Arabia. Ann had once helped him by editing one of his publications in English. He was now employed in this Qatari university where I had just begun to work. His wife and daughters had returned to Jordan for the girls' higher education, so he was now living alone. Many years earlier, as a disillusioned academic, he had fled Iraq over political issues that endangered his life.

Working Abroad with Purpose

In Doha, Qatar, we renewed and furthered our friendship over dinner at a local restaurant. As he shared his discouragement over lack of job security, he welcomed my offer to pray for him right on the spot. On another occasion while having dinner together, in response to my summary of the core gospel truths, he responded with "That's different . . . that's wonderful." After three months of these occasional meal appointments, he readily agreed to meet weekly at his apartment for Bible reading and discussion. Those meetings went on for five weeks until the day he drove me to the airport for my return to the United States. I can still hear him say while reading from the Sermon on the Mount, "This is the way it ought to be, praying in secret and not for show." Another time he commented, "No one ever taught me these things before." This came from a man who had taken his PhD at a major American university but had never heard and understood the Christian gospel. Six years later, having learned he had eventually found a teaching position in Jordan to rejoin his wife and daughters, I was eagerly looking forward to meeting up once again during a short-term volunteer teaching assignment in Jordan. While searching for his exact whereabouts, I was stunned and saddened to learn of his recent unexpected death. I never learned how that came about but found comfort in recalling his many expressions of admiration for what we read together about Jesus in the Gospels.

In Hong Kong came a further surprise when a Chinese believer introduced me to several Afghan merchants with whom he had tried to share his Christian faith. He took me to an apartment where several of them lived, and soon I was involved in a network of Afghan merchants. These Afghan men based in Hong Kong were selling lapis lazuli stone from Afghanistan to jewelers throughout Asia. They readily responded to my invitations for dinner at our home. Sometimes I took them on car rides for leisure activities outside the city in wooded areas where we found swimming holes and an occasional pack of roaming monkeys. They appreciated the fact that my young son and I were folks who appreciated their culture, and I was a rare westerner who was able to converse with them in Farsi, a language similar to their own Dari. These were tough, daring fellows who had fought the Russian invaders and had settled their families for safety in Peshawar, Pakistan while they were away at war or on business. One of them still had a Russian gun shell lodged in his forearm. And they were devout Muslims, once asking at our home in which direction the sun would set so they could posture themselves correctly for their prayers. Many times, Ann cooked food, Afghan-style, for these men. As we sat around a spread-out tablecloth on our living room floor, pots of steaming food were passed from the kitchen for the evening meal together. A few showed interest in a Farsi New Testament on our lamp stand, and one took a copy for himself. This and many others were opportunities we had never dreamed of having simply by taking up employment far away from our own homeland.

9

Confronting Issues in Language Learning

THE NEED FOR LANGUAGE LEARNING

A COMMITMENT TO TENTMAKING involves a readiness to learn another language. First, a tentmaker must determine what language is actually used by the anticipated fellow workers, probable neighbors, and likely acquaintances in the new living situation. That is, the language that will be needed in small shops, government offices, and centers of recreation. Generally, the tentmaker's own first language, even if English, is not the widely shared local language. Many local people may have some competence in the tentmaker's native language, and some may even be learning it in school or at a language institute, but it is not their mother tongue, the language that most resonates in the heart and mind. The newcomer's own first language may seem to serve well enough with some of the first contacts, but a command of the local language greatly expands the range of meaningful conversation with local friends and contacts. The local language not only helps to forge relationships, but it is the one through which the quite unfamiliar concepts of the Christian gospel can most readily be grasped for the first time.

Confronting Issues in Language Learning

Lai explains, ". . . Nothing is more critical for enhancing our long-term viability and effectiveness in ministry than our fluency in the language. Language fluency and cultural sensitivity are keys to becoming an insider with our adopted people."[1] Accordingly, he recommends taking a full-time language course for a year or more, though not all BAM proponents view language learning to be so critically important.[2] Scott Moreau, professor of missions at Wheaton College who was reared in a missionary home, observes a worldwide trend that bears upon the language issue for both present and future tentmakers. He points out the worldwide increasing use of English. He writes, "One of the realities of the urbanization and globalization of the world is that English has been moving toward being a 'world' language (though with countless variations) . . . It is true that in certain locations language learning does not always occupy the core strategic role that it played prior to contemporary times."[3] Once the tentmaker concludes that in the long-term perspective the local language must be learned to fulfill ministry objectives, its acquisition must find its place in his/her priorities regardless of how difficult its mastery appears to be.

In Iran, we learned that fluency in Persian, often called Farsi, was essential for meaningful conversation with the vast majority of people we would meet, particularly outside academic circles. So we began having language lessons in the early weeks once we were settled in our own apartment. In the Asir Province of Saudi Arabia, our sphere of contact and friendship consisted mainly of other professors and their families, mostly Arabs from surrounding countries. The majority of these had earned their advanced degrees in Western countries, often the United States or England. They were highly proficient in English, and many of the wives were also comfortable using English. Except for villagers who hawked goods in the open bazaar, most of the shopkeepers and workers in this remote part of Saudi Arabia were foreigners from Egypt, Yemen, Pakistan, and India. They represented a range of first

1. Lai, *Tentmaking*, 125.
2. Johnson, *Business as Mission*, 40–41.
3. Moreau et al., *Introducing World Missions*, 19–20.

languages and dialects, and many used basic English as needed. So, in that context, our learning basic elements of Arabic was mainly for directing a taxi, shopping in an open market, and for a token gesture of identification with the local culture.

In Hong Kong, thanks to the British tradition, English was widely used in the sphere of higher education where much of our friendship and ministry developed. We found it helpful to learn enough Cantonese to give directions to a taxi driver or to shop in outdoor markets for fresh produce. However, many Chinese friends we met in the English-speaking churches we attended, as well as most of our neighbors, easily turned to English in social situations involving outsiders. In Moldova, my work and primary contact was with local teachers of English who were largely trilingual, knowing Russian, Romanian, and English. Simply being able to greet politely, work with numbers, and make simple requests in Russian was sufficient for the purposes of our five-month stay. However, had we been aiming to reach common people in Moldova, a command of a local language would have been necessary, as would be the case among the common people in Saudi Arabia, Qatar, Azerbaijan, and even much of Hong Kong.

THE LANGUAGE LEARNING TASK

Even prior to entering the target locality, people now have many ways of getting a head start in learning a second language—particularly the sound system, high frequency expressions, and the most basic vocabulary. Many foreign languages are taught in home country universities, and several proven self-study courses are available for purchase online from companies like Pimsleur and Rosetta Stone. The latter now offers materials in at least thirty major languages. While still in the homeland, for at least a taste of the language and culture, a person can sometimes find speakers of the desired language among the international students at a major university or among the salespeople in ethnic shops in certain quarters of a large city. At the same time, reading books on the history and culture of the chosen country or region is an early step toward cultural adjustment.

Once in the context of overseas employment, the language learner is surrounded by speakers of the desired language. Some foreign employees are offered a short course in the local language, perhaps arranged by one's own employer, as I enjoyed in Hong Kong. Often a newcomer can find a local language institute with day or evening courses in the local language. Hiring a personal tutor, even one with limited teaching experience, can be a valuable resource in learning pronunciation and just how things are said in daily life. Whatever the local community may offer by way of language courses and tutors, Brewster and Brewster's guidebook for the language learner gives step-by-step procedures for tackling a new language. Their work, entitled *Language Acquisition Made Practical: A Comprehensive "How-To" Book for Learning Any Language*, is known by many as the "LAMP." Their detailed directions are engagingly illustrated throughout to reinforce the text. Of course, the experience of living with a local family in the new community, as the newcomers' own family situation may permit, yields huge returns in learning both the local language and culture.

Before going to Iran, I was able to take a university course in beginning Persian for two semesters while I was taking courses for a graduate degree in the teaching of English as a second language. This gave me some basic competence in the language but limited ability to hold an extended conversation. Once settled in Iran, I continued learning by means of lesson books with audio tapes, a small tape recorder, and an untrained but resourceful young tutor. Apart from the materials in the lesson book, I developed the habit of jotting down whatever I wanted to say in specific situations but couldn't and brought it back to my tutor for the next session. Putting to use whatever I learned from the tutor in similar social situations soon afterward seemed to help seal it in my memory for recall when next needed. Ultimately, I found that my foreign language proficiency became a treasure that I valued when in Iran, but even for years after leaving that language community. To this day, what Farsi I learned and continue to use serves me well in reaching out to Iranians, both university students and refugees, in the Chicago metropolis. It's especially valued for home Bible studies with Farsi speakers.

Most monolingual adults facing the daunting task of learning a foreign language cringe at the thought of doing tedious practice drills, memorizing lists of vocabulary, and making embarrassing mistakes in spite of their best efforts. Yet, language learning for a determined learner promises uplifting experiences and an ongoing sense of personal achievement. I remember how the most basic elementary greeting in the foreign language lit up the face of an unsuspecting native speaker of that language. I recall my deep sense of accomplishment when I successfully answered simple questions for a small purchase in the market. My first successful short telephone exchange without resorting to English was, for me, a huge breakthrough. Months later, and into the second year of learning while holding a job in that community, I realized that entire two-hour long tutoring sessions were being conducted without any reference to my first language. As a tentmaker, what a taste of victory came with the first spoken prayer in a public worship service. Eventually a spoken testimony, a short Bible talk, and a one-to-one inductive Bible study with a local inquirer followed. Language learning, although sometimes a struggle, had become a sure road to emotional highs along with the occasional embarrassing mistake that later made for a hilarious story.

Everyone is capable of learning a second language to some level of practical use given sufficient emphasis, determination, and humility—that is, willingness to be like a child again, making lots of language mistakes while putting it to use. Obviously, some acquire a second language more quickly and easily than others, and learners vary in their most comfortable means of acquiring the new sounds and grammatical patterns. Adult learners have much to gain from discovering and favoring their own preferred learning style in both choosing a language course and in guiding the role and techniques of a language tutor. For example, one learner wants grammar rules and patterns to memorize, and another prefers to approximate those patterns through guessing and personal discovery. One processes new material better through aural intake while another understands and retains better what is presented in written form. Some are comfortable with the ambiguities of larger chunks of the new language, but others are flustered without clear translation of what they are encountering piece by piece. As for strategies in speaking situations outside the classroom, some boldly experiment with the bits and pieces they have learned while others plan carefully and work hard to overcome hesitancy and fear of blundering. The whole learning process is greatly accelerated as an individual learner realizes how he or she learns best and capitalizes on that strength. Further, each learner must have reasonable objectives over time in terms of the speech functions they want to perform with the new language, ranging from asking and answering basic questions, telling stories, summarizing past experiences, and explaining difficult concepts.

Some adult language learners make remarkable progress on their own even without the help of study materials or a tutor. I have been amazed when observing Iranian refugees in Turkey who gain functional fluency in Turkish, a totally different language from their own, through attentive listening and imitation without any previous exposure to that language. Their success largely comes from determination to learn so they can obtain some kind of temporary livelihood in their new cultural setting as they wait years for ultimate passage to some Western country. In general, the learner who has realistic short-term and long-term learning objectives, awareness of his/her most comfortable way of learning, determination to put to use what is being learned without fear of making mistakes, and willingness to improvise where there are gaps in learning is sure to keep moving toward higher levels of proficiency.

10

Relating to Existing Ministries

EITHER PRIOR TO OR following entry to the host country community, a tentmaker is apt to learn of other Christian ministries already underway in the tentmaker's new situation. These might be an outreach to students at a nearby university, Bible translation and literature ministry, follow-up ministries to Christian radio or television broadcasts, church planting efforts under a missionary agency, or even an outreach ministry launched by an existing local church. At the same time, the majority of the people in the community have little, if any, understanding of the gospel. Many pockets of the community are practically isolated from the gospel message, and a tentmaker's workplace and immediate neighborhood may be untouched by those existing ministries.

As tentmakers my wife and I both benefited from and contributed to one or more of these existing Christian ministries in most places we resided. In Iran, we found mission agency initiatives in church planting, ongoing work in Bible translation, educational institutions in various states of allegiance to their founding purpose, hospitals with a Christian identity founded years earlier by Christian missionaries, and churches established by missionaries of an earlier era. In some of these we met workers who encouraged us and even included us in roles of ministry. In Hong Kong,

Relating to Existing Ministries

there were scores of existing ministries, both church-based and parachurch, including student work in the universities, and city-wide evangelistic crusades featuring notables like Billy Graham and Louis Palau. The crusades drew people we had befriended and gave us an opportunity to follow-up new believers. At English language churches established mainly for expatriates in Iran, Hong Kong, and Qatar I was able to help in preaching and teaching. Early in our residence in Iran, as well as in Moldova, I preached and taught in local churches with the help of a translator. In those two settings we found a supporting role in the ongoing work of the International Fellowship of Evangelical Students. In some places we lived, I volunteered to give workshops for teachers at Christian ESL teaching centers while Ann volunteered to serve on school boards. These opportunities to serve arose from the initiative of others quite apart from effort on our part. We simply got involved by being available when asked.

How was it that after less than a year in Hong Kong we were put in charge of the planning and oversight of a semi-annual weekend church retreat on an outlying island? That came about in association with a leading Anglican church in Hong Kong. As a family of four we had been regularly attending the Sunday services at this church early in our residence in Hong Kong; we decided to take advantage of the church's upcoming retreat at Cheung Chau, a quiet outlying island with seldom used retreat accommodations. We heard it would allow us to leave the usual noise, rush, and pressure of the big city in exchange for a leisurely weekend of recreation, Bible teaching, and singing. Ann and I, as well as our children, participated in all the activities over the weekend and thoroughly enjoyed it. A week after returning, I wrote the Cheung Chau Parish Weekend Committee a letter of appreciation and included a few suggestions for future retreats. Not long afterward, the vicar wrote me that as the members of the committee were discussing leadership for future retreats, "Believe it or not, your name was immediately raised . . . I would like, now, to ask you whether you would be willing to be the chairman of a committee to instigate the . . . creative planning you spoke of and organize the weekends."

Accepting the invitation, but just for the upcoming retreat, Ann and I got involved in planning the program, assigning roles, and providing promotion for the event. In the process, we found our way deeper into the lives of this multinational congregation and eventually into other outreach-oriented ministries of this strategically located church. We had simply gotten on board of an ongoing church-based ministry until our personal outreach ministries in Hong Kong took shape in other directions.

As a rule, a tentmaker has much to gain by contacting people involved in any ongoing Christian work, meeting them personally, and, when appropriate, observing their work firsthand. Through this personal contact, not only does the tentmaker learn the background and shape of other ministries, but the tentmaker also develops trust with others and gains the opportunity to explain his/her own role and vision. In some cases, he or she may find an opening to meet a need in the other's ministry. A tentmaker does not come to compete for local trainees, ridicule the work of others, or duplicate what is already being done well. The primary aim is rather to lead people to Christ and help see them develop into mature disciples.

However, there is need for sensitivity in exploring established organizations and their ministries. In some overseas situations there may be churches with ministries newly independent of foreign resources, control, and accountability. The unannounced appearance of a new foreigner with aspirations for personal ministry may provoke questions in the minds of the custodians of those established ministries. They may wonder whether the newcomer comes with an agenda appealing to local congregants and trainees for some new undertaking elsewhere. Any newly gained autonomy may be under careful watch. Hesitancy to embrace the foreign newcomer may arise from circulated stories of well-funded far away Christian movements with grandiose designs and big budgets to reach into their own community to set up something new. So, in view of the plethora of mission agencies and megachurches in the West that may be working out global strategies, it may follow that the less the tentmaker appears beholden to any foreign-based initiative or sponsor, the greater the likelihood of ready acceptance and trust. While some tentmakers may be warmly welcomed, others may face latent reservations and a cool reception that may change only with the passing of time.

As a newcomer in the city of Shiraz, Iran, after having lived in Tehran for three years, we enjoyed a welcome into the sole visible Iranian church, an Anglican congregation founded by British missionaries many years earlier. The church was under the capable leadership of an Iranian vicar, formerly a Muslim, who had received his theological training in India. This vicar was warm and welcoming from the outset. He encouraged my participation in church activities and eventually in its outreach ministries. After several months, he once included me in the series of speakers for a Persian Good Friday service, asked me to lead Bible studies among the church youth, once arranged for me to lead a Bible study for a group of visiting Iranian Anglican ministers, and asked me to carry on individual Bible studies with local seekers, young men he himself had first vetted for sincerity. One long-term foreign resident observed that I was the first foreigner, or at least among the very first, that the vicar had so warmly received. I suspect that my employment at the local university and my not being under the direction of any foreign organization were factors contributing to the initial welcome and ongoing trust.

11

Benefiting from Local Employment

A TENTMAKER'S ORDINARY SECULAR employment in the local community serves in numerous ways to establish relationships with nationals and opportunities to share the good news of the Christian gospel. The jobs my wife and I held embedded us in the local culture and provided sufficient income that enabled us to adopt a standard of living comparable to that of our colleagues and neighbors. Beyond that, our jobs gave us an inside view of the local culture, helped us contextualize our Christian witness, reduced people's inclination to ask why we had settled in their community, and did much to preempt misperceptions of our overall purpose in their country.

Our jobs abroad put my wife and me, and our children as well, in a network of personal friendships. For example, an immediate colleague in my university department introduced me to a younger brother, a recent college graduate, who became one of my language tutors. Another brother of his chose to enroll in my section of a required English course at the same university. In time, we were invited to their parents' home for dinner, and in turn, Ann prepared a meal for that family at our home. It was with my immediate colleague, his wife, and the brother who tutored me that I had the most opportunity to share something of the person and

Benefiting from Local Employment

work of Jesus Christ. From an expanding network of relationships like this we as vulnerable newcomers found help in purchasing a second-hand car, settling terms with a housing agent, and negotiating the purchase of basic household items. In summary, a local job helps establish common ground and credibility with a host of colleagues, neighbors, and chance acquaintances.

Another example of what Ginter calls "serendipitous ministry"[1] occurred in our first months in Iran. One late afternoon an Iranian gentleman from a downstairs apartment rang our doorbell and introduced himself in good English. He explained that he had locked himself out and asked if he could simply sit and wait for his wife to return home from work. I gladly complied, sat with him, and soon learned he was working for Iran's Ministry of Foreign Affairs. While we were talking, he spotted on our tea table J. N. D. Anderson's edited volume, *The World's Religions*, which led to conversation about religious faith. Less than an hour after he had left to join his wife, he returned with copies of over a dozen English poems he had once written, asking me to read and share my thoughts on them. Later, as I read, I found several expressing a deep longing to know the Creator or Ultimate Being. One of them began and ended in the following way:

> I am willing to talk to you
> My Lord
> But are you willing to hear me?
> Or maybe you know
> What I am going
> To talk about . . .
> Misery and pains
> Of a troubled heart

Over the following months Ann and I met his wife, the friendship grew, and he began to read the Gospel of John. One day we coincidentally met out on the street, and he stopped to say, "Let me tell you what I found in John's writing that I like so much." He referred

---

1. Ginter, "Overcoming Resistance," 215–16.

to one of Jesus' discourses on intimacy with God the Father. On another occasion, he introduced his brother to us, arranged to have him come along for dinner at our home, and, as I recall, on his departure declared, "This evening in your home I have felt the presence of Jesus." Not long afterward, this friend was transferred to an Iranian embassy in Europe, and several years later with the overthrow of the Iranian monarchy we totally lost contact. I could not confidently conclude that our neighbor had come to a saving knowledge of Jesus Christ, much less claim a conversion to our credit. Rather, we could say we were neighbors whom he trusted, a trust that led to his receiving and reading the Gospel of John. Over many months he came to some understanding of the Christian teaching of salvation through the unmerited grace of God. What we could say is that as tentmakers we were strategically located, readily accepted by others, and often engaged in meaningful exchanges with the local people. We were privileged to plant the seed of God's word in many lives while we ourselves attempted to live gospel-oriented lives that they could see. It is God who in his time brings about the harvest so that one day "the sower and the reaper may be glad together."[2]

Local employment helps tentmakers demonstrate transparency and integrity among people who watch them settle into the local workplaces and neighborhoods. Regardless of how open or resistant to the gospel a host country and its people might be, the vocational role and daily conduct of a tentmaker in their own locality is evident to all. The income-generating job helps to dispel doubts or qualms about what motivates the person to take up residence in their community. We found that as locally employed tentmakers we had no need to conceal a foreign sponsorship, no need to explain a puzzling unknown source of income, no need to take on pseudonyms, or need to use coded language in electronic communications with friends back home. We certainly had no need to keep friends and churches that were praying for us in the dark about the exact country or city of our residence abroad. As tentmakers, we were not living with carefully guarded secrets and

2. John 4:36.

did not live in fear of embarrassing disclosures about who we were and what we were doing. Tentmakers need not experience what missiologists Patrick Lai and Rick Love call the "schizophrenia"[3] of maintaining a duel identity that can be so burdensome, that is, being a missionary in one context and something else when asked by nationals in the country of residence.

Authentic tentmakers can offer a straightforward, satisfying explanation of who they are and what they are doing. They have been hired to provide a local service through a hiring process that gave little attention, if any, to their personal values, philosophy of life, or religious beliefs. In fact, the tentmaker in a Muslim majority context benefits from the fact that he/she is following the historic Muslim practice in that the most religiously devout "are expected to earn their livelihood in some . . . honourable occupation,"[4] as historian Bernard Lewis notes in discussing Muslims' lack of a formal priesthood. Lai and Love, reflecting on their own past experience, follow Lewis's train of thought: "In Islam, many imams (like the apostle Paul) work regular jobs in the community. As a missionary, I would be perceived as a trained terrorist. As a Christian businessman, I am nothing noteworthy."[5] Clearly, in many sociocultural settings, local people see nothing out of the ordinary in a person having secular employment for a livelihood while being actively engaged in religious pursuits.

In an article startlingly entitled, "Why I Am Not a Missionary,"[6] Larry Sharp, after forty years of formal missionary service, describes how he decided to discard the missionary label in favor of the label of business person and educator. He opted for a more acceptable identity among the people he would meet in different countries. It appears he had come to understand that nowadays, in non-Western contexts, the term missionary signals—at best—a good-hearted dispenser of charity to the underprivileged, but to some people it connotes being a person who proselytes

3. Lai and Love, "Integrated Identity," 337–38.
4. Lewis, *Middle East*, 187.
5. Lai and Love, "Integrated Identity," 349.
6. Sharp, "Not a Missionary," 478–84.

through subtle tactics for personal reward, or worse, one who is a spy or even a trained terrorist. Such notions are certainly detrimental to acceptance, friendship, and trust. Consequently, the employed tentmaker, as a devout Christian, is better off not assuming the term "missionary" that too easily triggers misunderstandings and unhelpful stereotypes.

A long-time friend of mine, after living and serving in Iran for many years, explained via personal communication his own change of identity from missionary to English language instructor. He lived among people who, early in a friendship, felt free to ask personal questions about another's livelihood and financial situation. He wrote:

> A usual question was "How much do you make each month as a salary?" The second question immediately followed, "Who pays your salary?" I tried to evade that one by saying a bunch of people in America who think very highly of you pay my salary. They would answer, "Oh, so you mean a church is supporting you!" With an affirmative answer, right away a heavy wall or curtain would descend and conversation might end.

The writer could go on to explain how different it was during his later years as a bona fide tentmaker in another part of the same country where it was evident to all that he was earning his salary by teaching in a local university. During his years teaching university students as a tentmaker, he was able to complete his long-term project of translating the New Testament into modern, colloquial Persian for eventual distribution shortly before the Islamic revolution forced him and most westerners out of the country.

In addition to the possibility of a gross misunderstanding about a Christian worker's motivation in advancing religious beliefs is the danger of total misperception of what he or she is actually doing in the host country. I recall hearing three single missionary women who lived together in a large Eurasian city sharing their thoughts. They were engaged in their required full-time language learning. One referred admiringly to a personal acquaintance who held a job as a nurse: "She has no problem explaining to local people what she's doing here." These three young women feared at times that despite their best efforts to explain their role, some observers suspected they were really involved in the sex trade.

Another serendipitous opportunity to share my faith occurred in Qatar, and upon reflection impressed upon me the universal applicability of the tentmaking model. Three weeks into my one-semester appointment to teach academic writing at the leading university in Qatar, and newly settled into one of the spacious eight-room, two-storied villas for foreign employees, I was startled to hear my doorbell ring late one night. I turned on the porch light, opened the door, and there before me stood a stalwart man in Arab dress with two small children and a full-grown sheep at the end of a rope. He explained in English that as my immediate neighbor, he had noticed that the sheep he had bought for the approaching Eid al-Adha festival was always favoring my front porch, perhaps for the shade provided by the overhang. These were the animal's last hours, he explained, and it would be a good thing for the sheep to be kept as content as possible. So, he asked, could the sheep enjoy the cool of my porch under the overhang at the coming break of day and the morning heat? I agreed and allowed him to tie it to a porch railing for the night. Neither of us foresaw the animal somehow getting loose during the night hours, fouling up the walkway, and in the morning finding refuge in another part of the large walled-in expatriate community, only to be cornered and escorted home.

Yet, my neighbor had more in mind in approaching me. That evening under the porch light he proceeded to describe in detail the meaning of the festival sacrifice, the way Abraham was ready to slay his son in obedience to God, and how that son was spared. After I responded with my understanding of the story and something of its meaning for today, he insisted that we soon meet again to discuss these things further. The next day the poor sheep went the way of millions of other sheep on that festive day, but at my neighbor's home for tea I learned that he had come with his family to Qatar from Pakistan. He was an experienced F-16 fighter pilot, had once received training in the United States, and was currently contracted to serve in the Qatari Air Force. Above all, he was a devout and informed Muslim. Despite our being poles apart on the way of salvation, we were able to talk respectfully at length about our faith commitments on several occasions because we were neighbors and employed ultimately by the same emir. That gave us common ground, literally in that expatriate complex, and an initial mutual understanding of why we each were residing far from home. In fact, he, as a practicing Muslim employed outside his homeland with eagerness to spread his Islamic beliefs, in a sense, was practicing a Muslim type of tentmaking, though I never thought to probe into his awareness of that. Yet, his job away from home that planted him in a residential complex, where at least a few others did not share his faith, gave him occasion to reach out to "unbelievers." He welcomed open doors to explain his faith even as I would. Was he aware of how it was Islamic Arab traders and craftsmen and their families that long ago took up residence in countries of the Far East, built mosques, practiced their faith, and carried on their businesses and crafts, and in so doing helped plant the Islamic faith in those regions?

12

Identifying Provision for Medical Care

A TENTMAKER WILL DISCOVER in the host country what provisions God in his sovereignty has arranged for routine medical care and emergencies. This is particularly important for workers who are unaffiliated with a missionary society and employed by a purely local institution or company, not an international firm or government agency. Regardless of the quality of medical services available in the target country, before leaving the home country, the tentmaker should visit his or her doctor for a thorough physical exam. Before my wife and I left for Iran, our personal physician not only gave us physical exams but ordered us immediately to have many immunizations by injection. Hours after that clinical visit, we ached in all our limbs as we loaded a rental truck with furniture and personal items for storage. But we were thankful for our doctor's concern and foresight. He also saw that we understood, or even had with us, what we might need for treatment of some possible illnesses. While at that time neither of us was on regular medication, years later, a personal physician helped us get the six-month or year's supply of the medications we needed since we could not assume comparable medications were available where we were settling abroad. We learned later that it might have been wise also to have asked our physicians if he/she would have minded being available for any needed urgent consultation from abroad.

A tentmaker, like all expatriates abroad, does well upon arrival to register with the home country's nearest consulate to benefit from its mission of looking after citizens residing in the host country. Consulates provided us with practical information on local dangers, health risks, and information on treatment centers accessible to us as foreign residents. Most likely, tentmakers going abroad for work with a large international firm or a governmental department in the target country are sure to be given orientations in which all matters of health and medical services are thoroughly covered. We attended this kind of orientation when preparing to go abroad in educational programs under the jurisdiction of the U.S. State Department. We were sometimes updated and guided further by consulate staff after our arrival. Workers with large companies or programs under a foreign government's auspices are sometimes given medical treatment at in-house clinics with contingencies for evacuation for any critical medical condition.

The quality and accessibility of medical care abroad varies hugely from region to region. Undoubtedly, some countries in the Far East offer state-of-the-art medical care, often at a fraction of the cost the same service costs in North America. In some countries where public health services are poor, the private clinics set up for employees of big businesses, like those set up to serve diplomatic personnel and their dependents, are not open to unaffiliated persons. However, in countries that were once pioneered by medical missionaries, foreign residents might find Western-trained doctors still serving in those missionary hospitals open to all who come.

We saw firsthand something of the vast difference in the quality of medical services available abroad. For our needs as a family of four, we had no reason to doubt the adequacy of the medical services available in British-run Hong Kong. There were both good public hospitals and Christian hospitals with good administration, capable staff, and qualified doctors. In Iran, public

Identifying Provision for Medical Care

hospitals were acceptable, and our first child was delivered in a Tehran public hospital. In the outlying provinces, there were a few hospitals established many decades earlier by Christian missionaries. These continued to offer services to all who came, and our several visits to these for treatment met our expectations. On the contrary, in Moldova and Azerbaijan we were cautioned about the capability and quality of service we would receive at the public hospitals. Instead, we were advised to look to any foreign operated clinic open to us or, if need be, know what country in the region to reach by air travel for admission to medical services of good reputation. In Moldova, stories circulated of patients needing surgery who, after the initial diagnosis, were given a list of paraphernalia and medicines needed for the required procedure and told to buy and bring the purchases to the hospital. The hospital simply did not stock these items. Foreign residents several times warned us, not just in jest, that Moldova was not a good place to get sick. This was the state of the local medical services at that time.

In a Middle East provincial capital, foreign faculty members had grave doubts about the care given at the one public hospital. The wife of a Palestinian colleague gave birth to her first child in that hospital. Friends had to bring her meals since the hospital did not provide food service for in-patients. Misgivings were furthered by stories of foreign doctors working there with forged or questionable licenses for practice. Amusingly, that one hospital was the place applicants for a driver's license were required to go to donate blood unless they were over the age of forty. A colleague explained how the process made him extend his sleeveless arm through an eight-inch hole in a partitioning wall for someone, unseen to him, behind the wall to draw his blood.

In that city, Ann and I learned our own best recourse for treatment of minor medical conditions was to visit the friendly Pakistani doctor at the university's small clinic set up for faculty members and dependents. On one occasion, we chose to consult with a Western physician friend some thirty miles away at a military hospital. He and several other Western doctors practiced medicine there for military personnel and the foreign experts who were giving instruction on the use of imported military weaponry. We did not have direct access to that facility, but were given personal attention by our friend who worked there.

In some places we lived abroad, we faced an extra measure of hazards and health risks. We had to cope with many drivers on the road, both licensed and unlicensed, and some underage, who gave little attention to street signs and speed limits. Many of them had little or no experience driving under difficult road conditions, and few were restrained by the thought of being stopped by the police. Police officers, we observed in some places, might let a driver off the hook with the passage of a few bank notes. Tailgating at speeds in excess of eighty mph seemed to be for some a national sport. Unsurprisingly, we heard of road accidents resulting in serious injuries and deaths. To this day, we remain thankful to our prayer supporters for our daughter's safekeeping on those hazardous roads on the daily sixty-mile round trip to her school in a Saudi-driven van carrying the foreign children.

We observed in some communities that safety standards commonly observed in most Western countries were quite unknown, and standards that were posted were widely ignored. Walkways were often poorly lit at night, leaving uncovered manholes or obstructions hard to see. Falling objects from tall buildings were a danger. Food purchased in supermarkets or even served in restaurants could be expired or poorly preserved, and tap water was unsuitable for drinking. As for dietary needs, along with the many tasty national dishes we came to love, at times we had to take steps to avoid nutritional deficiencies due to seasonal scarcity of greens and other vegetables.

As a family and later as a senior couple without accompanying children, we were always thankful to God that we had no critical illnesses abroad and were always able to find the medical services we needed. We suffered only a couple of falls causing non-life-threatening head injuries, and apart from child delivery we had only a single hospitalization, one stemming from a case of exhaustion. A stubborn chest infection was effectively treated by antibiotics, supplied by our medical doctor friend. Colds and flu, as well as digestive disorders, were treated by ordinary household remedies.

Only God knows the many times we were kept safe from serious accident or illness through his special providential care. Once in a newly rented apartment in Baku, Azerbaijan, I got a glimpse of that special care. I had begun to explore a basement stairway in near darkness in a newly occupied apartment, but after several cautious steps, I hesitated and turned back. The next day in a shaft of light from an open door I saw that with another step or two I would have plunged through an uncovered opening in the floor into a cavity below. God provided wonderfully for us in so many ways during those years living and working abroad.

13

Having Income on Extended Home Stays

LOOKING OVER A COUPLE of our old missionary prayer calendars with names of thirty or more missionaries that Ann and I followed in prayer for years, we are reminded of case after case of long-term departures from the field of work. Some had to return home for just several months for an emergency, some for a year or two, and others for an indefinite period, if not permanently. One young family far along in their first term on the field returned to the U.S. for an indefinite period due to critical medical needs of a newborn. Another young couple with three small children returned home, after counseling, for an extra year of rest and renewal of vision to overcome the effects of unusually stressful field work. An experienced missionary couple felt it best to return to their home country for at least a year to get extended help for their troubled adopted child as well as for some personal medical needs. Another mature couple left their field of work permanently after thirteen years, with deep misgivings over policies of their sending agency. A younger couple left their field work after five years to pursue graduate studies and a change of vocation after a series of disappointments stemming from the host country's imposed restrictions. In all these cases, the missionaries themselves, their

Having Income on Extended Home Stays

agencies, and even many of their supporters had to deal with questions about their ongoing material needs while home from their field of work for an extended and often undefined length of time.

Missionary careers of thirty years or more without major disruption are now exceedingly rare compared to that of missionaries of the mid-twentieth century and earlier. This may be due in part to a different mindset among today's missionary candidates compared to those of earlier generations. Yet, today's ease of travel facilitates a return home for specialized medical treatment, for assistance or extensive care of aging parents, or for further education to upgrade one's expertise for the overseas ministry. In addition to these personal reasons for a time of retreat are involuntary disruptions resulting from actions of hostile governments, political instability, and even outbreak of war. All in all, many conditions, personal or political, warrant or demand a return to the homeland, usually with the intention of returning to the field after a supposed amount of time or the passing of a host country crisis.

A Christian worker who is forced or chooses to return home for a lengthy or undetermined length of time is faced with questions about a source of continued income. For a traditional donor-supported worker, regardless of the sending society's policy on this matter, the customary donations for support may taper off, and those that continue may come with some awkwardness as months turn into years. A tentmaker who returns home for an extended period responds to this predicament much like any professional in the homeland handles termination, whether unexpected or after some premonition. In preparation for such a predicament, a tentmaker is wise to keep any professional license or certification current. An up-to-date resume showing previous employment, both the recent work done abroad and any previous employment replete with references, is key to finding a new source of work for a one-year position or longer.

Pursuing an online search combined with strategic networking within one's professional community are promising avenues to new homeland employment. Of course, one's exact field of expertise and how the work experience outside the homeland is perceived, whether positively or negatively, bears upon how readily an applicant might find work in a competitive job market. Ideally, the tentmaker has qualifications and a work history in a field of wide-ranging application. Yet, qualifications and skills in some fields of expertise that served one well abroad may need to be refreshed, amended, or updated when reentering the field in the home country. It may be necessary for a tentmaker to settle temporarily for a different line of work, even unskilled work, until a desired position is found. Certainly the churches that have upheld the tentmaker in prayer would be possible sources of leads for both the desired kind of work or for temporary alternative employment.

During our tentmaking career, Ann and I twice returned to our homeland for a three-year period. We once returned home so I could undertake PhD studies that focused on adult learning and literacy in Iran. Another time, we were forced to return home due to the ongoing Iranian revolution. In that case, after eight months of job searching, I was hired for a university position coordinating a language-teaching program for international students in another part of our country. For that particular position my personal experience in the Middle East was viewed as a valuable asset. The new job gave opportunity for personal ministry among a new set of university colleagues and among some of the students, particularly those who were among the first to come from China in pursuit of graduate-level American education. At that time, this same university housed the only center for Afghanistan studies in the United States. As a result, I was soon enjoying friendship and exchanges with a number of Afghans, some having been dignitaries who had fled to America upon the communist takeover of their homeland. Three years later, we returned as a family to another position abroad and resumed our tentmaking career for eleven more years.

14

Facing Unpredictable Material Crises and Retirement

A TENTMAKER WILL SEE God's faithful material provision in times of unexpected need through both proactive steps and God's unpredictable interventions. Like all who live in obedience to Jesus Christ, the tentmaker looks to the heavenly Father for material needs as well as for the spiritual. However, there are steps a tentmaker can take to be prepared for an unanticipated financial crisis. A personal crisis abroad might arise from serious sickness, costly accident, injury, fire, or foul play. The possibility of these episodes is greater in many places tentmakers tend to go. Accordingly, he/she should have potential resources in mind for coping with such challenges. If the person or couple has had at least a few years of prior work experience before venturing abroad, there may be some available savings to draw upon. In certain cases there may even be benefits or help from the overseas employer. Close friends in the host country may provide a loan, a supporting church back home may want to help financially in special times of need, or one or more of the individual prayer supporters might be able to respond to the need with a loan or gift.

We took several steps to prepare for both probable and unknown financial challenges. In case of a major medical need beyond the expertise available in the hosting country, we maintained a high deductible catastrophic health insurance policy offered by an alma mater for stateside treatment. For both emergencies, as well as for our eventual retirement, we learned to systematically invest in mutual funds while working abroad. This was our partial substitute for much of the social security benefits we would lose upon retirement for the years we did not have an American employer paying into that plan, nor we ourselves doing so voluntarily during those years. We learned how to benefit from American mutual funds from a pioneer missionary friend involved in Bible translation when visiting us in Hong Kong. We are glad for the portion of social security benefits we now do receive by virtue of past employment with InterVarsity and the years of work at two American universities. Ann's social security benefits were similarly reduced. The steps we took to compensate for those losses in retirement have thus far proven quite adequate for our current needs and ongoing ministries. All in all, should our own foresight and best efforts in this area yet prove to be insufficient, we continue to trust the heavenly Father for his unpredictable ways of providing for his followers' material needs.

The Scriptures provide the grounding for the tentmaker's confidence that God provides in all seasons of life. At a time when communication with far-away supporters or a quick money transfer was not possible, the apostle Paul experienced God's sufficiency and grace in times of dire need. In his letter to the church in Philippi, a church that sometimes helped him financially, he wrote from prison that he had learned the secret of contentment in both times of plenty and times of want (Phil 4:10–13). Clearly, at all times Paul instinctively trusted God, who through Jesus Christ encouraged and enabled him to fulfill his life's calling. Undoubtedly, his reliance upon God was buttressed by his thorough acquaintance with God's wondrous ways recorded in the books of Moses, the Old Testament historical accounts, and the Psalms of David. The God who supplied what his people needed in times past was the same God who provided for him and his companions.

Facing Unpredictable Material Crises and Retirement

The Scriptures show that God's ways of intervening to meet people's needs are often extraordinary. For the wandering Israelites, God provided bread from heaven and water from a rock (Exod 16 and 17). For Elijah, God brought bread and meat by way of ravens, and a little later, by way of a poor widow who gave him the little she had, only to find that her jar of flour and jug of oil yielded a continuing supply (1 Kgs 17). Elisha witnessed one poor widow's single jar of oil filling many jars to enable her to satisfy the terms of her heartless creditor (2 Kgs 4). In New Testament times, after teaching a large crowd for many hours, Jesus chose not to send them away hungry, but rather multiplied a few loaves and fish to feed more than 5,000 on one occasion and similarly over 4,000 on another (Mark 6 and 8).

God sometimes used natural means in remarkable ways to meet pressing need as seen in the lives of the apostle Paul and his traveling companion, Silas. Once, when hungry and hurting after beatings and imprisonment, Paul and Silas were given a full meal in the home of a dramatically converted jailer (Acts 16). On another occasion, after being stranded on a Mediterranean shore due to a disastrous shipwreck, Paul and friends were given food and hospitality by the sympathetic chieftain of a coastal town on the island of Malta (Acts 28). No doubt these recorded episodes of God's material provision for Paul are only a few of many more not recorded for us. The God of the ancient prophets, the God of the tentmaking apostle, and the God of today's tentmaker is the same, and he is one who provides.

While often not in the dramatic fashion of the cited biblical examples, we too experienced God's timely unanticipated interventions. When we returned to the United States from a chaotic Iran being swept by revolution, a relative gave us rent-free use of his vacant home. We were unemployed and glued to news reports coming from Iran, some portraying massive crowds chanting "Marg bar Amrika" (Death to America). Increasingly, we pondered what all this meant for our future and our deep commitment to the Iranian people. It gradually dawned on us that we would have to find work and settle down somewhere, at least for a year or two, to regain a pattern of family life as we waited for guidance on possible further work and residence abroad. We faced many questions. Should we resume working with InterVarsity requiring donor support, do outreach ministry as a staff member of a large American church, or return to academic work at a university? There were months of reflection and waiting on God while searching for a U.S. based job. When it came time to choose, I felt constrained to maintain a secular footing, even for ministry in the United States. I accepted the position of academic coordinator of an intensive English language program for international students on a midwestern university campus. It was later that the somewhat mystical-minded, foreign-born director of that program who hired me shared that to him the final sign that I was the right man for the open position was the fact that he and I had been born in the same year on the same day. Somehow, he found meaning in that, and I had a job. Amid all the uncertainties, God answered our prayers by providing a job and a place to live and carry on a similar ministry.

Yet, through all of this we faced considerable financial stress. Our savings had been depleted by the completion of the PhD degree just over a year earlier. Now, having to make a down payment for the purchase of a sixty-year-old frame house, making monthly mortgage payments, tending to urgent home maintenance, all while caring for two children, ages eight and two, stretched us to the limit. We struggled to make ends meet. Ann got a part-time job at minimum wage at a nearby florist, but half her earnings went straight to child care. At the end of each month, we were relieved those times we still had as much as a two-digit bank balance.

God knew our situation and intervened on our behalf to supply all that we really needed. I recall receiving in the mail a check for six hundred dollars as part of the inheritance of a distant relative. Another time we received a check from an insurance company for seven hundred dollars to settle for the rear-ending of our tired old Plymouth, a car we were about to donate to charity. One Sunday, most surprising of all, on our return from church, was finding an envelope attached to our front door. It was from our insurance company's agent who that morning had gone down the block, house-to-house, writing checks to clients for recent hail damage. We ourselves were unaware of any damage to our roof, but we opened the envelope to find a four-figure settlement.

In our overseas situations, as a family, we similarly witnessed God's gracious interventions, often through his people, to meet sudden needs in ways we could not have foreseen. In Tehran, weeks after our first child was unexpectedly delivered by Caesarean section, one of our home churches in America deposited in our Stateside bank account all that we lacked in covering the hospital bill. A year prior to the outbreak of the Iranian revolution, while I was in Iran without my family gathering data for a doctoral dissertation, I sustained a politically-inspired break-in by a group of extremists who left the message, "Go home. Never come back to Iran at all. Think about your family"—the last sentence in large letters written in bright red ink. The local police authorities inspected the scene for evidence, and a Christian friend provided a temporary haven across town until I could arrange for a more secure place to stay while continuing the research. How my critically needed and irreplaceable data was spared is an amazing story of God's goodness when replaceable items like my passport, return air ticket, and Persian Bible with teaching notes were all carried off in my own portable typewriter case leaving the typewriter behind. Nothing of real monetary value was taken. God had provided a shield of protection for both the dissertation and the researcher.

In Saudi Arabia, I was informed that a phone call had come through for me from the United States to inform me, the only son of my widowed mother, that she had suddenly become critically ill. My Saudi employer granted me a release to fly home several days before the end of the semester while Ann with our two children remained behind for their own scheduled later flight. A day after I left, Ann recalls how a Muslim neighbor woman, having heard of my hurried departure, came to our apartment door offering Ann a handful of bank notes to be sure her needs were met during her husband's absence. In retrospect, it occurs to us that often in those trying times we faced as tentmakers, it was local colleagues, local friends, and local authorities who were God's means of his gracious provision which, along the way, strengthened bonds of friendships with the people God had placed around us.

15

Limitations and Logistics

AN ASTUTE TENTMAKER FACES squarely some inevitable limitations and logistical factors in planning and launching a tentmaking ministry. These considerations help a missions-minded person move from the world of ideals to the realities of daily life.

FACING TIME LIMITATIONS

A critical factor in the ministry of a tentmaker is time management, or better, management of activities in light of time constraints and overall priorities. People everywhere speak of being too busy to do all the good things they wish to do. They say they are too busy to read books, follow the news, get acquainted with neighbors, or stop to help a stalled motorist. Christians often admit to the same frustration and add to the list that they are too busy to keep up old friendships, too busy to attend prayer gatherings, and too busy for a habit of personal Bible reading with meditation and prayer. Tentmakers are not immune to the same time squeeze. In addition to the tasks mentioned above, they add the challenge of making time for language learning, cross-cultural friendships, and systematic reflection leading to thoughtful reporting for prayer supporters. They sooner or later face the reality that they cannot force everything into their daily routine as they had hoped. This human limitation demands hard choices and prayerful prioritization.

The apostle Paul twice states one basic principle that a tentmaker can apply in selecting and prioritizing his or her most essential activities. In his first letter to the church in Corinth, Paul wrote: "All things are lawful for me, but not all things are helpful" (1 Cor 6:12; 1 Cor 10:23 esv). Tentmakers must repeatedly ask themselves which activities are most helpful for accomplishing the ministry objectives and which are expendable, that is, just not very helpful toward fulfilling those objectives. They must also ask themselves what might be the proper allocation of time to the activities they decide to be essential. These, of course, are in addition to tending to spiritual nurture, physical well-being, family needs, and job requirements which must not be neglected. Determining the proper amount of attention to the essential spheres of activity requires prayerful consideration and periodic review.

FACING BIOLOGICAL LIMITATIONS

One relevant variable among all people, including tentmakers, may be less subject to fine tuning. I once arranged a breakfast meeting for two university engineering students interested in tentmaking to help them learn from an experienced missions-minded senior engineer who often spent months at a time for his company in limited-access countries. One of the first questions the well-travelled engineer asked the two students was, "How much sleep do you fellows need to function effectively?" He had in mind the limitation of energy that everyone has to face. That question pertains to the number of hours a day a person has for his or her work and ministry. While few people have the constitution of a Thomas Edison or a Margaret Thatcher to work so hard and long on just a few hours' sleep, there is a practical difference in what people can undertake between those who are fine with six or seven hours of sleep a night versus those who need eight, nine, or more. Bodily needs and energy levels benefit greatly from the Lord's design of one day in seven for rest. Yet, a person's energy capacity on through the successive days of the week is a factor to consider in determining whether to pursue a tentmaking career or some other means of cross-cultural ministry abroad.

PATTERN OF WORKLOAD

More a matter of logistics is how the tentmaker's work routine can coincide with the envisioned ministry to colleagues and acquaintances. Job routines vary in both their intensity and flow of activity. Some jobs involve more concentration and stress, and some entail longer hours. Job workloads may vary seasonally or cyclically. Some jobs offer flexibility in establishing a work pattern with the main concern simply being the completion of a certain amount of work in a given time span without a specified routine. In the field of teaching, typically there are periods of greater demand balanced by times of lighter workload, or more free time and flexibility during summers. When offered a particular job in the target country, it is wise to consider the routine it will likely involve and consider its impact on both the intended ministry and family life. Ultimately, a tentmaker's pattern of outreach at the workplace and neighborhood will be impacted by the work load pattern of the job. Fortunately, most jobs have some ebb and flow in the workload. Recognizing this variance helps to preempt hasty feelings of failure at those times job duties seem to encroach upon family needs and outreach activities. Times of lighter workload usually follow.

To generalize from my own work experience in different teaching jobs, both abroad and in my home country, the first year in a new position is always more stressful and challenging as the worker has to figure out local expectations, output standards, available resources, and established practices. In the field of education, usually a new job meant designing or revising curriculum for the first class of students, but that same material was often carried over to the next time the class is offered with only small revisions and additions. That understanding about the first year in many kinds of jobs can help prevent premature negativity about the tentmaking experience. As the worker gains a rhythm in a new job, patterns in home life, personal friendships, and intentional ministry naturally unfold. The tentmaker should not need more than a year to develop a significant focus on evangelism and discipleship, not several years or more of strenuous preliminary work developing a BAM business undertaking, as experienced BAM practitioners acknowledge.[1] Within a year, perhaps just within months, a tentmaker can be comfortably settled into the flow of job requirements in phase with proper attention to family needs and ministry to others.

Married tentmakers can work out a kind of division of labor for periods of time in implementing priorities when just one of the two is employed. In our second year abroad, when Ann stopped teaching to care for our first child, she and I each assumed changes in daily routine. Ann had less time for language study and social contact outside the home while I assumed a few new household duties while maintaining my usual teaching load at the college. I retained daily contact with students and colleagues and continued language learning while Ann's main contact with local people, apart from those in small shops within walking distance, was with visitors for whom she provided hospitality. In retrospect, I now see I did not adjust my work routine and role at home as much as I could have for her benefit, but she practiced the grace that enabled our outreach ministry to continue at a high level. Also, in the following several years only I had employment outside the home, and she spent most of her time at home caring for our two children. She more than compensated for the limited time I spent with our children. Now, decades later, I attribute a lot to her unwavering attention to the children, and the faithfulness of our prayer supporters, that our two children now in adulthood are Christ followers who speak positively of their upbringing and life abroad. The fact that Ann and I had shifting roles for many of our years abroad no doubt reflects the same phenomenon that couples experience in our homeland as children enter the picture.

---

1. Lai, *Business for Transformation*, 33, 41, 151, 179; Johnson, *Business as Mission*, 63.

Limitations and Logistics

CONCEPTION OF MINISTRY

Tentmakers are sometimes questioned in the homeland on how they can possibly have outreach ministry when holding a full-time job. The answer, in part, includes something about how the tentmaker learns to minimize less helpful activities and maximize the opportunities that come while always making good use of discretionary time towards his/her objectives. However, the answer also has to do with how one perceives ministry and measures it. Should ministry be quantified only in terms of hours or days in pronounced evangelistic or Bible teaching activity? A tentmaker is more inclined to conceive of ministry as engagement in a society or sub-culture with a Christ-centered mindset and way of life. In the course of daily activities serving others, he/she seizes every timely opportunity for personal witness, informal discussion of biblical truth, and interaction on honest questions.

On work days, the tentmaker aims to join fellow employees for lunch instead of lunching alone or habitually with the same one or two like-minded friends. Like all employees, the tentmaker as a rule has one or two days off from work every week giving time for both family activities and outreach ministry. In countries where there are more holidays, both national and religious, than occur in the home country, a tentmaker often involves colleagues and neighbors as well as family in plans for those days. Allotted annual vacation days also figure into the equation of life and ministry. Further, year-round a tentmaker makes a lasting impression on any occasion of emergency or special need of a colleague or friend by taking personal time or, as permissible, time off the job to assist, console, and offer prayer. All in all, tentmakers believe that a job in a non-Christian or secular environment is in no way an obstacle to ministry. Rather, for the person with a trained eye and ready heart for ministry the job is a vehicle of opportunity.

Time after time I thankfully saw how my job opened up avenues of friendship and personal witness that I doubt I would otherwise have had. When working as head of the language center of a university in Hong Kong, I once had to assess cohorts of students' levels of need for English in classroom learning and research projects in the fields of biology, chemistry, and physics. My consultations with the Chinese faculty members in these departments of science led to new friendships, especially with two physics professors. In the weeks and months that followed, I often met one or the other off campus for lunch, and our conversations easily got into matters of faith. One in particular heard me share more than once about our need for a Savior in the face of sin, corruption, and human shortcomings.

I well recall one discussion I had in 1989 a few days after scores of mainland Chinese protestors had been cut down by gunfire from Chinese soldiers in Beijing's Tiananmen Square. Hong Kong residents everywhere were glued to their TV sets following news reports of the ongoing carnage. When my physics professor friend and I settled down for lunch at a Hong Kong restaurant, his first words to me were something like, "You are right, evil is real and we cannot control it." That led to a discussion of humankind's need for salvation and God's provision through the gospel of Jesus Christ. Years later, on a follow-up visit to Hong Kong, he volunteered to me, though not yet a Christian, one more member of his larger family had chosen to follow Christ. For sure, he had become fully aware of the Christian gospel, Christ's claim on our lives, and the gospel's practical impact on personal life. Accordingly, the tentmaker's outreach ministry can best be measured in terms of trusting relationships, strategic imprint on others by word and deed, and moments of clear explanation of the gospel to attentive individuals. These are things that cannot be reduced to a count of hours spent in strictly Christian activities.

16

Concluding Remarks

A PERSONAL REALIZATION

MY OWN VENTURING INTO a tentmaking career may have been conditioned far more than I once realized by the example of my father. Having come to the United States from a large wheat farm in Saskatchewan, Canada, at the age of nineteen with a high school diploma and some knowledge of electricity through a correspondence course, my father first settled for a temporary unskilled job. Then in 1928 at the age of twenty-one, he was hired as a trainee by the International Time Recording Company of New York at a wage of forty cents per hour. This company eventually changed its name to IBM. For many years my father worked for that fast-growing company, and in the early 1940s was a district manager in Michigan. At that point, when I was a small boy, he decided rather than continuing as a cog in a large organization that often required relocating, he would rather venture into the purchase and operation of a small company servicing and selling electric motors. This was a move with far greater risk than staying with an expanding IBM, but one that gave him more flexibility and control over his personal and family life.

In the new undertaking, each day brought challenges with no clear pathway or directives to follow. He had to rely on his own past learning, his own good sense, ingenuity, and determination. Yet, he lived in communion with God. I recall many times his reciting Proverbs 3:5–6 (kjv): "Trust in the Lord with all thine heart; and lean not on thine own understanding. In all thy ways acknowledge him, and he shall direct thy paths." His small company eventually grew to have two, three, and more employees whom he personally trained. Each day my father might have wondered if there would be enough incoming work to keep employees busy. Would the incoming repair jobs be manageable, or might they prove to be extraordinarily difficult and unprofitable? And eventually, at the end of each week, would there be enough bank balance for payroll? At the same time, I am sure, he pondered how his faith might be made known to worldly-minded employees, associates, and clients. Years after Dad's passing, I read accounts in his small personal diary about hardened business associates gaining softened hearts to listen to the story of the gospel that had brought meaning and direction to his own life and family.

What I learned from Dad was to honor God in all of my work, to delight in work well done, and to carry on my work in communion with the living God. Glimpses of Dad on his knees in prayer at bedside before breakfast at the start of a new day impressed on me the key to Christian living wherever I might be and whatever my job would be. Dad's venture in a small business and my teaching in an overseas university were both adventures with God who delights in his people and faithfully delivers on his promises. I am sure God found great pleasure in both Dad's work well done in a noisy machine shop and in my own best efforts in teaching and researching in classrooms abroad. Awareness of God's watchful care over us was a constant source of encouragement and perseverance as I with my wife and children spent so many years of our lives serving the Lord Jesus abroad.

Concluding Remarks

A TENTMAKER'S QUALIFICATIONS

Missiological literature contains various statements on personal qualifications required of a tentmaker. David Tai-Woong Lee, one of the primary mission leaders of South Korea, summarized four basic requirements of a tentmaker:

> First, you must be able to nurture yourself spiritually . . . Second, you must be competent in your chosen vocation. Third, you must be able to adjust emotionally to the stress of living in your host culture. Fourth, you must have practiced skills in witnessing to other individuals and nurturing them in their spiritual growth.[1]

There is no substitute for self-nurture through regular thoughtful intake of Scripture. Your daily habit of Bible reading and prayer, both alone and, if married, with your life's partner, enables you to keep your inner life uncluttered and focused on the priorities that you have prayerfully worked out. As for competence in your field of work, ideally, if you are not already established in a vocation, you can begin searching into appealing fields of study that can lead to fulfilling employment in service to people and society. The choice should match your personal inclinations and the probable job market in your envisioned country or region of interest. Once you settle on a field of work and have had the necessary training, you need to gain practical experience in that field for credibility and greater appeal to potential employers. Your chosen field of work is not merely a means to another end, but a stage on which you are serving God, his creation, and the social order he has established.

The ability to make cultural adjustments that Lee points out can begin to develop on the home front in urban contexts through your involvement with refugees, international students, or by just hanging around people in an urban ethnic community. Lee's last critical requirement is experience in witnessing to people about the gospel and discipling them in the faith. Tetsunao Yamamori, missiologist and past director of the Lausanne Committee for World Evangelism, phrases this qualification as being "trained

---

1. Lee, "Cross-cultural Servants," 32.

in long-term and low-profile evangelistic skills."[2] That is, having the ability to share the gospel and means of Christian growth with individuals over a long-term relationship. This requirement often begins with the helping hand of a more experienced believer through mentoring and partnership, but must never stop developing and adapting to new situations. As a tentmaker you must have a deep conviction that God desires to work through you and that God is already at work in your target community preparing people to encounter the gospel in ways yet to be discovered. That conviction will sustain you in times of waiting and periods of work and witness when you may see little visible results.

In addition to Lee's four qualifications is working out some arrangement for team work in the targeted country. Some tentmakers are fortunate to set out as a team or set out to join others they have already come to know in the field. A candidate may be in communication with an established missionary agency that recognizes and encourages a measure of cooperation with tentmakers in one of their fields of work. Just how formal any tie with a mission agency or organization designed to assist tentmakers can be depends, in part, on the host country's restrictions on religious affiliations as expressed in a work contract or any published guidelines for expatriates. Some countries or employers may explicitly prohibit membership in a political or missionary sending organization. To sign such a contract and disregard the stipulation is both risky and unethical. Whether or not to have a formal tie with an agency also depends upon the personality and bent of the tentmaker. For tentmakers with contracts having no stated religious restrictions, and who work out a formal tie with a mission agency, one cautionary note is to beware of letting organized gatherings for both social and devotional purposes take the place of deep involvement with nationals, both Christians and non-Christians, that the tentmaker has come to reach and serve. The tentmaker who comes to a host country to reach the hearts and minds of nationals must keep them in his/her active social circle.

---

2. Yamamori, "Foreword," VI.

Concluding Remarks

One personal trait that benefits the work and career of a long-term tentmaker, particularly those from North America, is readiness to accept a possible lower profile in homeland church gatherings or missionary conferences by not having the formal identity of a missionary. Particularly among evangelicals in the United States, traditional missionaries are accorded special favor and affirmation for their dedication, service, and sacrifice. Although the tentmaker has the same underlying motivation and cross-cultural experience that most traditional missionaries have, his/her secular identity can give most church people the impression of being more of an ordinary layperson whose calling is not so special. That perception may be reinforced by the fact that the tentmaker foregoes the missionary label and many of the customary ways of a donor supported missionary like fundraising envelopes, use of magnetic prayer cards, and periods of home service. Accordingly, among people with little or no understanding of the tentmaker's secular identity and distinct strategy, the tentmaker may lack the special aura that characterizes traditional missionaries. The tentmaker who understands this phenomenon gladly accepts it while attempting to educate church people of the strategy and role of a tentmaker. It is of crucial importance that missionary advocates in the homeland come to understand the importance of the tentmaker's secular identity and its important implications. Their appreciation of that strategy and their use of appropriate terminology in communicating with the worker and with others about that overseas worker help to safeguard the tentmaker's ministry.

In addition to a tentmaker's essential personal qualifications is the great benefit of having a sense of engagement in an adventure. The tentmaker has chosen to ply what is often an unmarked pathway with many God-given opportunities and provisions to be discovered along the way. Learning how God answers prayer and delivers on his promises is an enriching experience. A book on tentmaking, as you are now reading, provides signposts and insights on the pathway, but your own venture and discoveries along the way will bring about your own account of God's faithfulness in your venture for the advancement of his kingdom and the glory of Christ. Through it, you gain a story to tell others about how vocational expertise can be carried and transplanted in another part of the world, rooted there, and bear fruit for God. That personal story, in time, will inspire others to take up a tentmaking adventure.

AN ENDURING MENTALITY

Long-term tentmakers who eventually resettle in their home country are apt to retain some distinct tentmaker characteristics. This is often the case whether the return home is to another full-time job or to retirement. The tentmaking career portrayed in this book is one that holds personal evangelism as a high priority, and that deeply ingrained concern for the salvation of others remains in the years that follow. When returned to the homeland, whether in a workplace environment, neighborhood setting, or elsewhere, sharing the gospel with others is not just something the tentmaker used to do. Having learned to work out that priority in many different situations abroad, it is only natural to work it out again in the familiar home territory. The priority to share the gospel was never a matter of mere compliance to a job description or responding to the prompts of a team leader. The habit of daily looking to God for guidance for new occasions to share the good news remains strong. The tentmaker continues to believe that in every gathering of people are at least a few who will respond to friendship and Christian witness. Some tentmakers as returnees are bent on reaching out to newcomers to the tentmaker's homeland like refugees and international students. Some, as personal finances and health permit, may even plan occasional visits to the former host country, the place of so many personal friendships.

As a tentmaking couple we returned to the United States after resigning from our positions in Hong Kong, ten or twelve years before the typical age of retirement. During our last months in Hong Kong, I interviewed for positions at two universities in the United States, and only a few weeks prior to our planned departure I received an offer of a full-time position at a public university to teach in a graduate-level TESOL program. The return to our homeland involved a new setting of activity, but only small changes in our pattern of activity. Two years after settling in our new home, Ann was hired for the headship of a small developing Christian elementary school in the same community. Early in this new setting, we were having Sunday afternoon Bible studies for international students, in addition to teaching Bible classes at church. We witnessed our daughter's university graduation while we encouraged our son through his high school years and into college. Yet, the appeal to help overseas was still strong. During those years of employment in our home country and two years into our retirement I received three overseas assignments, two for a five-month period and one for ten months, to train English teachers in Qatar, Moldova, and Azerbaijan under the U. S. Department of State. These shorter stints abroad were very much part of our tentmaking experience.

After these assignments, further overseas trips were typically solo undertakings for a month at a time, mostly at personal expense, to do volunteer work assisting missionary endeavors in programs teaching English as a foreign language, and training nationals hired to teach in those programs. These trips were to Tajikistan, Kyrgyzstan, Greece, the Philippines, Jordan, and Egypt. Since 2011, I have made annual visits to Turkey to help in Bible teaching in churches composed of Farsi speaking Iranian refugees. In our own home community we have hosted numerous gatherings of Farsi speaking refugees, university students, and local Farsi-speaking acquaintances for Bible study in Farsi, their first language. Retirement years have also included scores of trips to universities in Chicago to meet and befriend international students, especially those from Iran. So much of this homeland activity is parallel to what we did for years while employed and living abroad. Indeed, tentmaking, once begun, develops a mentality that lives on as long as God provides strength and resources to reach out to others.

A WAITING OPPORTUNITY

In today's world there are numerous people groups whose members will likely never personally enter into friendship and dialogue with a living witness to Jesus Christ unless a Christian takes up a job alongside them or establishes residence among them. That is true across much of the Muslim world, which today is less accessible to traditional missionaries. This is the case also in less restricted communities of the Majority World, even in some highly developed non-Western countries. In Hong Kong, where there has been missionary activity for over one hundred and fifty years, there are people in business circles and working-class communities whose members fail to have a meaningful relationship with a devout Christian. In Hong Kong, I recall seeing enclaves of unreached people like members of the Nepali Gurkha brigade, their dependents, and the community of Afghan merchants selling to jewelers precious stones mined and brought from their homeland. These people are approachable by tentmakers who work among or near them and reside in their communities. The opportunities awaiting a new generation of tentmakers are vast. Twenty years ago, Yamamori, in the foreword to the book *Working Your Way to the Nations,* called for more tentmakers: "Tentmaking is a subject of strategic importance to world evangelism. The concept is biblical, historical precedents abound, and today's mission context demands it . . . Tentmakers must be deployed, and in large numbers."[3] That call is even more urgently needed today in light of the increasing restrictions on traditional approaches in many regions of the world.

Venturing abroad as a tentmaker entails some risk taking in the face of the unknowns of a new community, language, and workplace. Lai, in writing about tentmaking, concludes, "Research shows that tentmakers are creative and enjoy taking risks."[4] Yet, the tentmaker's risks are not totally unlike risks taken by most people when making major decisions, be it for employment, relocation,

---

3. Yamamori, "Foreword," V.
4. Lai, *Tentmaking,* 228.

Concluding Remarks

long-term investments, large purchases, or certainly in regard to marriage. People take risks in the hope of some probable positive outcome that makes the perceived risk well worthwhile. Approximately 4,000 years ago, Abraham chose to accept the risks and unknowns involved in God's call, and he obediently left his familiar surroundings and extended family to discover what God had planned for him. God calls people today, including tentmakers, to face unknowns when entering unfamiliar territory. The unknowns, however, one by one, become things familiar as they serve God and neighbor in those strange places. For certain, the person who is motivated to spread the gospel knows that the venture to move onward is in keeping with God's revealed plan for the advance of his kingdom among all nations. The short-term risks involved become manageable in the light of God's promises and presence.

The discussion of twelve areas of a tentmaker's undertaking, chapters 3 through 14, represents what I with my wife learned about tentmaking both before and after the tentmaking term gained much currency. These twelve components of tentmaking provide approximations of what a new generation of tentmakers can attempt and expect. Possibly, when beginning a new job overseas, some things are not at all up to expectations. The workload may seem too heavy, the initial housing problematic, arrangements for children's schooling disappointing, or contact with the local people may seem elusive. Such things are the givens for your own discovery of God's provisions and interventions for needed adjustments in the initial situation. For example, after a few months in Hong Kong, we found God's way for us to move from cramped and noisy accommodations to a more suitable location for both family and ministry. In Iran, after my first year of teaching, I realized some advantages of working at a smaller, more friendly college than at the more prestigious Tehran University. We found God's way to make that change after the first year. Similarly, through your own discoveries of God's leading and answer to prayer, you may be able to add insights to improve upon the guidelines and steps found in this treatment of the way of a tentmaker's living purposely abroad.

Working Abroad with Purpose

Making a long-term commitment to cross-cultural ministry of any kind is a serious and life-shaping decision. I had made a commitment to serve abroad during my college days long before Ann and I were married and left our homeland together to set up household in Iran. When we set out, we had agreed to stay the course for an initial five years, come what may. As it turned out, the Iranian Islamic revolution capped our time spent in Iran at just five years, much to major personal disappointment. Having returned home to contemplate our next steps, the possibility of eventual return to Iran was fading. While waiting, we considered work in a church-based ministry in the homeland, student ministry on secular American campuses, or temporary employment in some American industry. The outworking of that earlier lifelong commitment to serve abroad seemed so unclear. But we sensed God's guidance to continue using the same workplace skills that served us so well for our livelihood and ministry abroad. Accordingly, after a few years of university work in our homeland, we returned overseas to continue cross-cultural ministry as tentmakers. We learned that the skills that made for tentmaking abroad served us equally well for our needs and ministry in the homeland. The tentmaking model gave us a remarkable flexibility in the face of the often-changing situations of our contemporary world. By this model, we have been able to enjoy work as a vocation for which we were created while being serious adherents of our Lord's Great Commission. We trust many others choose to follow this model of working abroad and advancing the gospel among unreached people.

Appendix
Resources for Tentmakers

GLOBAL INTENT (formerly Global Opportunities): Based in Fort Myers, FL (https://intent.org). On the drop-down menu, choose 101 which leads to FAQ'S—Frequently Asked Questions. See "How can Global Intent help you?" There it reads, "Global Intent helps you find where God wants you to serve by helping you with your job search, training materials and programs, and linking you with missionaries and tentmakers overseas, whenever possible."

INTERSERVEUSA (formerly Bible & Medical Missionary Fellowship): Based in Upper Darby, PA (https://interserveusa.org). Terri Taylor, Director of Communications, writes: "Interserve can offer you: (1) Connection with an established team to provide support, (2) Training in cross-cultural communication, including expressing your faith effectively, (3) Engagement with multi-cultural partners who can help you adapt and overcome cultural blind spots, (4) Wise counsel from field leaders who understand the importance of partnership and servanthood, and (5) Security training, crisis management and a theology of suffering."

MARKETPLACE & DEVELOPMENT ENTERPRISES (MDE): Based in Farmington, MI (https://buildmde.com). Select "What We Do" for a detailed description. President and CEO Mark Canada writes: "MDE is a service organization dedicated to partnering with and supporting believers who desire to utilize their vocational or

Appendix

business skills and experience in unreached communities. Our goal is to help connect those believers with opportunities and resources that encourage and enable them to use their skills and passions to take the presence and message of Jesus to others through the natural relationships that flow from working and living in authentic ways in those communities."

Tentmakers International (formerly TIE): An association of national movements (www.tentmakersinternational.info). They offer training for tentmaking through their network of resourceful people. Through individual membership in TI, a person gets (1) A newsletter with updates on tentmaking, (2) Updates on job opportunities, (3) Access to available TI trainers in the member's country, and (4) TI teaching materials. The website lists national representatives in thirty-seven countries (November 13, 2018). Under the tab "Jobs," it reads: "We process job opportunities by collecting and distributing opportunities through member organizations . . . Also we invite resumes and we will try to match with appropriate requirements in various countries."

Bibliography

Allen, Roland. "The Case for Voluntary Clergy." In *The Ministry of the Spirit: Selected Writings of Roland Allen,* edited by David M. Paton, 135–189. Grand Rapids: Eerdmans, 1960.

Brewster, E. Thomas, and Elizabeth S. Brewster. *Language Acquisition Made Practical: Field Methods for Language Learners.* Colorado Springs: Lingua House, 1976.

Cox, John. "The Tentmaking Movement in Historical Perspective." *International Journal of Frontier Missions* 14 (1997) 111–17.

Ginter, Gary. "Overcoming Resistance through Tentmaking." In *Reaching the Resistant: Barriers and Bridges for Mission,* edited by J. Dudley Woodberry, 209–18. Pasadena, CA: William Carey, 1998.

Green, Michael. *Evangelism in the Early Church.* Grand Rapids: Eerdmans, 1970.

Hamilton, Don. *Tentmakers Speak: Practical Advice from Over 400 Missionary Tentmakers.* Duarte, CA: TMQ Research, 1987.

Harnack, Adolf. *The Mission and Expansion of Christianity in the First Three Centuries,* vol I. 2nd ed. Translated and edited by James Moffatt. New York: Putnam, 1908.

Johnson, C. Neil. *Business as Mission: A Comprehensive Guide to Theory and Practice.* Downers Grove, IL: InterVarsity, 2009.

Lai, Patrick. *Tentmaking: Business as Missions.* Waynesboro, GA: Authentic, 2005.

———. *Tentmaking: Business for Transformation: Getting Started.* Pasadena, CA: William Carey, 2015.

Lai, Patrick, and Rick Love. "An Integrated Identity in a Globalized World." In *From Seed to Fruit: Global Trends, Fruitful Practices and Emerging Issues among Muslims,* edited by J. Dudley Woodberry, 337–53. Pasadena, CA: William Carey, 2008.

Latourette, Kenneth Scott. *A History of the Expansion of Christianity, vol. 1: The First Five Centuries.* London: Eyre & Spottiswoode, 1938.

Bibliography

Lee, David Tai-Woong. "Cross-cultural Servants." In *Working Your Way to the Nations,* edited by Jonathan Lewis, 27–40. Downers Grove, IL: InterVarsity, 1996.

Lewis, Bernard. *The Middle East: A Brief History of the Last 2,000 Years.* New York: Scribner, 1995.

Lewis, Jonathan, ed. *Working Your Way to the Nations.* Downers Grove, IL: InterVarsity, 1996.

Martin, Danny. "History." *Tentmakers International,* http://www.tentmakersinternational.info/index.php/history1.

Moreau, Scott, et al. *Introducing World Missions: A Biblical, Historical, and Practical Survey.* Grand Rapids: Baker, 2009.

Sharp, Larry. "Why I Am Not a Missionary." *Evangelical Missions Quarterly* 48 (2012) 478–84.

Siemens, Ruth. "What's Tentmaking?: Work Abroad – Make Disciples." *Global Intent,* accessed September 18, 2018, https://intent.org.

Yamamori, Tetsunao. "Foreword." In *Working Your Way to the Nations,* edited by Jonathan Lewis, V-VI. Downers Grove, IL: InterVarsity, 1996.

Wilson, J. Christy Jr. *Today's Tentmakers: Self-support: An Alternative Model for Worldwide Witness.* Wheaton, IL: Tyndale, 1979.

www.ingramcontent.com/pod-product-compliance
Lightning Source LLC
Chambersburg PA
CBHW070926160426
43193CB00011B/1591